Reclaiming
the
Oral Tradition
of the
African Baptist Church

DAVID W. SPARKS

EDITORIAL CONSULTATION: STEPHEN ERIC DAVIDSON

◆ FriesenPress

One Printers Way
Altona, MB R0G 0B0
Canada

www.friesenpress.com

Copyright © 2024 by David W. Sparks
First Edition — 2024

Author Photo By: Deacon Olusegun Odusanya

ISBN
978-1-03-831271-6 (Hardcover)
978-1-03-831270-9 (Paperback)
978-1-03-831272-3 (eBook)

1. RELIGION, CHRISTIAN CHURCH, HISTORY

Distributed to the trade by The Ingram Book Company

Dedicated to the Memory of Mother
Olive Mae (nee Thomas)
who taught me how to pray.

Table of Contents

Acknowledgements

This project would not have come to fruition were it not for the many individuals who encouraged me and assisted at various stages. I want to express thanks to the *Baptist Historical Committee* of the *Atlantic Baptist Convention* for providing start-up funding for this initiative, the *Historical Committee* of the *African United Baptist Association*, to the staff at the *Atlantic School of Theology*, the *Woodlawn Library*, the *Vaughan Memorial Library*, (in Special Collections), the *Black Loyalist Heritage Centre*, the *Nova Scotia Public Archives*, the Black Cultural Centre of Nova Scotia, and the individuals I interviewed for this project (most of whom are now deceased). Special thanks to Stephen Eric Davidson and Dr. Glenn Wooden for editing the manuscript and offering helpful suggestions. Also, I am thankful to the many friends and family (whose names are too numerous to mention) for their encouragement throughout this project.

"To go back to tradition is the first step forward"
-African Proverb

Introduction

The purpose of this research is threefold: to revisit, reclaim, and revive the oral and religious tradition of the African Baptist Church (ABC). The ABC in Nova Scotia was first established by the Rev. David George, a former slave, who was among the 500 Loyalists who sailed from Charleston, South Carolina, to Nova Scotia in November of 1782. In 1783 George would be joined by 3,000 recently freed enslaved Africans arriving in Nova Scotia at the end of the American *War of Independence*. While David George is credited with founding five churches in Nova Scotia and one in New Brunswick (Shelburne, Jones Harbour, Ragged Island (now Lockeport), Preston, Halifax, and Saint John, New Brunswick), the research does not confirm that all six churches practised the oral tradition, or whether they were all ABC. What is certain is that the church established in Preston would continue the oral tradition well into the twentieth-century. (More will be said about David George and his conversion experience in chapter Two.)

By *oral* we mean the practices, customs, beliefs, and folkways of a people and community that are passed on by word-of-mouth over several generations: from father to son, from mother to daughter, from mother to son. Because it is *oral*, it does not always get included in official church records. Moreover, by oral we mean that which is spoken and heard rather than what is read or written. It is what is felt rather than what is thought. That is to say, it is of the heart rather than the intellect. Based on the oral practices, it is what one must "do" rather than what one must "know".

Beginning in the slave cabins of the American South, it was not what was taught or believed, but what was *experienced* through a direct encounter with God that determined one's salvation. Yet despite their illiteracy and forbidden by law to read, enslaved Africans had a profound respect for the Bible. Biblical themes, events, and characters were an integral part of oral tradition. Scriptural passages and whole chapters were often committed to memory. Bible verses were seen in dreams, and words of hymns and spirituals told what was required for salvation.

There were attempts by other denominations to win the allegiance of the Black population in colonial Nova Scotia in the eighteenth-century. The Methodists, Anglicans, Catholics, and Presbyterians all vied to convert the Black community to their particular denomination. It was the Methodists, however, who presented the greatest challenge to the Baptist faith represented by David George. But it would ultimately be the African Baptist faith that triumphed and won the loyalty of the majority of the Black community. Many who may have been adherents of other faith traditions would eventually join the African Baptist fold.

Traditionally known as the Old Time Religion[1], remnants of a once powerful and dynamic oral tradition can still be seen in some African Baptist churches. The words of certain prayers once prayed by the deacons and elders can still be heard. The spiritual—the heart and soul of the African Baptist oral tradition—are still sung. However, not with the same enthusiasm and conviction. The popular altar call—the climax of an evangelistic message—has lost much of its appeal and is done less frequently.

The ring shout consisted of forming a circle around the church after the candidate[2] had given his/her experience. It is now done by forming a line in front of the church. Shouting with the candidate may happen spontaneously on any given Sunday while the candidate is waiting to be baptized. Shouting may continue even after baptism. On its church website, the East Preston Baptist Church describes this

---

1 The words *old time* first appear in the Book of Jeremiah, 2:20, and 6:16. It is the Hebrew word Olam, which literally means what is hidden or concealed. It can mean eternity, time immemorial, or without end. It is also a reference to God. We will show later in this work how the expression old time would become the oral tradition of the African Baptist Church.

2 The candidate is the designation given to the person who has been examined and approved by the church for baptism.

occasion as a "memorable tradition of the church", and what it calls the "rites of passage." This religious rite consisted of two weeks of prayer, fasting, and meditation before going down into the waters of baptism.[3] Today the rite of seeking and finding the Lord is no longer a prerequisite for baptism.

Traditionally the telling of one's conversion experience required the telling of one's *dreams, visions,* and *travels,* now requires only the giving of a testimony. And while historically the deacons were responsible for preparing the candidate for baptism, this task is now performed by church counsellors, or someone in pastoral training.

Several factors have contributed to the neglect and abandonment of the church's rich religious tradition. For one, there is the passing of the elders: those who were the keepers and pillars of the ancestral wisdom of the church's oral history. Hearing the accounts of their conversion experiences and how they *came* was deeply moving and humbling. As one elder stated: "We don't have anyone to teach the oral tradition." With the passing of the elders, many of the spiritual songs have been forever lost. The rejection and neglect of the spiritual wisdom of the elders has had a negative impact on the moral and spiritual life of the church.

Another important factor that has contributed to the loss of the church's oral tradition has been the

---

3 A Brief History of the East Preston United Baptist, p.3.
www.epubc.ca/about-epubc.

influence of greater educational opportunities. The argument is sometimes made that the oral tradition was God's way of bringing salvation to an illiterate people. But now that we are better educated, there are those who believe that such practices are out-dated and obsolete. "It was for such a time as then," stated one pastor. Though it is true that most of the former slaves arriving in Nova Scotia were illiterate, (this can be said about most people living in the eighteenth-century) still there were later genera-tions acquiring greater educational opportunities and the ability to read and write, still found themselves "seeking the Lord." Unfortunately, many African Baptists are still today ignorant and indifferent to their own faith tradition.

One of the most significant factors contributing to the demise of the African Baptist oral tradition has been the influence of Christian orthodoxy and White Protestant theology. Very early in its history the AUBA adopted the dominant, Protestant ortho-doxy and theology of its White Baptist counterparts. In seeking White approval and deference to "all things British", the ABC took on the trappings of organized religion, and hence the institutionalization of the Christian faith. The more fashionable, con-ventional approach to salvation, therefore, currently describes much of the structure and liturgy of the ABC. The loss of the church's oral tradition may help to explain many of the issues presently facing the church, whether it is division within the membership, lack of attendance, lack of leadership, or the absence of youth, all of these factors can be attributed to the abandonment of the church's oral tradition. I am convinced that had the church not abandoned its religious tradition, many of our fine young men who lost their lives through gun violence would still be alive; and many would not be incarcerated. Many of the AUBA's eighteen sister churches are now comprised of seniors and middle-aged adults. Young people are conspicuously absent. I am convinced that the break-up of the East Preston Baptist Church in 1998 (and again in 2008) could have been prevented had it not abandoned its founding tradition. The same could be said about Saint Thomas Baptist Church in North Preston—the largest church within the AUBA in terms of membership—that it would not be without a pastor had it not abandoned its oral tradition.

Today the process and orientation for new members consists of several weeks of religious teaching, consisting of certain prescribed literature and a booklet called *New Life in Christ* where the focus is on teaching rather than seeking. This more conventional approach to salvation may help to explain, in part, the lack of creativity and spiritual emptiness that describe many ABCs. It accounts for our present moral and spiritual crisis. (This theme will be further elaborated upon in the chapter on conversion). The loss and neglect of our religious tradition may also explain why many have left the ABC, and in some cases, have started their own churches under other denominational names.

One of the most adamant and consistent arguments given for opposing the church's oral tradition is that "it is not Biblical." But rather a folk tradition that has no theological basis. It must first be said that without tradition (i.e., that which is handed down) there would be no Christianity. Christianity began as an oral tradition before it took written form. Moreover, the early doctors of the church and the later Protestant Reformers of the sixteenth and seventeenth centuries did not wage battles against tradition, but against doctrinal error and false teachings; and against those traditions that contradicted the gospel.

Moreover, religious traditions have a sacred and divine origin whose beginnings are unknown—stretching back eons. The older a tradition is the more sacred it is believed to be. Religious traditions, therefore, transcend human constructs. They may have been transmitted by fallible mortals; they did not originate with them. Furthermore, we should not confuse the word *tradition* with traditionalism (i.e., the habitual and conventional way in which something has always been done). The latter is the adherence to doctrines and practices merely for tradition's sake. Traditionalism is opposed to change and is not forward-looking. The negative connotation of the word *tradition* (religiously speaking) therefore, is of recent origin.

Whether African Baptists will reclaim their oral tradition must wait upon the future. It is hoped that this ground-breaking research and examination will start a dialogue and a new appreciation for the church's sacred tradition.

Further, this paper will also attempt to show the theological and Biblical roots of the African Baptist oral tradition: a tradition of a once enslaved people that has gained recognition by reputable scholars as a field of study in its own right, and whose works I reference. Whether African Baptists will *reclaim* their rich religious heritage in the twenty-first century must wait upon the future. It will depend on having a dialogue in the spirit of humility and *agape* love!

Though the writer was raised in the African Baptist oral tradition, and has the advantage of experiencing this tradition first hand, every attempt has been made within my limited ability to be objective and true to the historical facts. The work begins with an examination of the efforts of the American colonists to Christianize their enslaved African population, and the slave community's reaction to those efforts. It will then examine the social, cultural, and religious impact of the *Great Awakening* upon the enslaved population. This will be followed by the conversion of David George and the arrival of the Black Loyalists in what is now Atlantic Canada. The next chapter will look at the arrival of the African Baptist refugees and Richard Preston in Nova Scotia, resulting from the War of 1812. This will then be followed by an explanation of the conversion process. The last chapter, the Epilogue, will recount the author's conversion experience, and how that conversion marked the rest of my life. It is also important to point out that this work is not about the history of the ABC proper, but about its oral tradition. All Biblical text will be taken from the New King James Version unless otherwise indicated.

Chapter One

The Christianization of the African Population

The seventeenth-century European powers believed that their colonization of the New World included the obligation, and duty, to Christianize both the enslaved and native populations. England, along with Spain, Portugal, the Netherlands, and France, "proclaimed missionary zeal as an important motive for colonizing the New world."[4] In 1660, Charles II issued the following instructions to the Council for Foreign Plantations, which read in part:

> *...And you are to consider how such of the Natives or such as are purchased by you from other parts to be servants or slaves may best be invited to the Christian faith, and be made capable of being baptized thereunto, it being to the honor of our*

---

4 Albert J. Raboteau, *Slave Religion: The Invisible Institution in the Antebellum South*, (Oxford University Press, New York, 1978), 97.

> *Crowne and the Protestant Religion that all*
> *persons in any of our Dominions should be taught*
> *the knowledge of God, and be made acquainted*
> *with the mysteries of Salvation.*[5]

English bishops issued challenges to North American colonists to follow the example of France, Spain, and Portugal in their missionary efforts to "evangelize the Indians and African slaves."[6] Several thousand of the enslaved were baptized by Catholic missionaries in North America before the Society for the Propagation of the Gospel (SPG)—a missionary agency of the Church of England—would begin its evangelization program at the beginning of the eighteenth-century. In Maryland in 1785, there were over three thousand enslaved who were baptized as Catholics.[7] Catholics were scattered throughout the United States, but they faced the same problems as their Protestant counterparts: a lack of clergy and opposition from slaveholders. Milton C. Sernett describes mission work among the enslaved as an "unglamorous task." He writes, "Even among the best-intentioned churchgoers there was a tendency to think of the plantation missionary as a practitioner of a low calling and a caste ministry."[8]

---

5 Ibid.

6 Ibid.

7 Ibid., 112.

8 Milton C. Sernett, *Black Religion and American Evangelicalism* (The Scarecrow Press, Inc., Metuchen, N. J. 1975) , 30.

Missionaries were not only needed to convert the 'Indians and Negroes', but the English as well. In 1724, Hugh Jones reported that North Carolina needed missionaries for the "Christening and Recovery to the Practical Profession of the Gospel great numbers of English, that have but the bare name of God and Christ; and that too frequently in nothing but vain Swearing, Cursing and imprecations."[9] How effective the missionary efforts were is hard to gauge. Still it can be argued that such efforts did have a positive impact on the enslaved community.

However, in the 1600s colonial plantation owners in America felt no obligation to Christianize their slaves. There were several reasons for this indifference. The primary reason was the fear that religious instruction, which would be followed by baptism, would free those enslaved. There was the growing belief in Britain that upon baptism an enslaved person should be emancipated. "The notion that if slaves were baptized, they should according to the laws of the British nation, and the canons of its church be freed was legally vague but widely believed."[10]

Despite assurances from colonial assemblies that baptism would not in any way threaten the legal right to "hold Africans in perpetual bondage" slaveholders' fears were not allayed. There was the added apprehension that baptism would make slaves less disciplined, and would encourage expectations of

---

9 Albert J. Raboteau, op. cit., 105

10 Ibid, 98.

freedom and equality. Masters also felt that because of the cultural and racial differences, Africans were incapable of Christian instruction. "It was the attitude of slave masters that Africans were '"too brutish to be instructed."' This objection was based on the '"linguistic and cultural barriers between African-born slaves and English colonials."'[11] For plantation owners, baptism was seen as an economic detriment. Their primary concern was to make as much money as possible rather than making Christians of their slaves. To counter the fears of decreasing profits, missionaries made the case that masters would benefit economically by their slaves being Christians, "for they are taught to serve out of Christian love and duty."[12]

Despite opposition by slaveholders to instructing enslaved Africans in the Christian faith, there were those who argued for the slave's conversion and his humanity on anthropological grounds. One such individual was Morgan Godwin, an English divine, who spent several years in Virginia. He never tired of reminding the English planters of their Christian responsibility to the enslaved: "Methinks that the consideration of the shape and figure of our Negroes bodies, their Limbs and Members, their voices and Countenance in all things according with other Men's...should be sufficient conviction."[13] New

---

11 Ibid., 100

12 Ibid.

13 Ibid, 101

England Puritan, Cotton Mather, echoed similar sentiments in his tract *The Negro Christianized*, in 1706: "Show your Selves Men, and let rational arguments have their force upon you, to make you treat, not as Bruits but as Men, those Rational Creatures whom God has made your Servants."[14]

Toward the end of the seventeenth-century, the British Parliament instructed the Virginia Assembly to pass laws allowing for the education of Indians and Negroes in the Christian faith. From pressure by American missionaries and officials in London, colonial legislatures passed bills that prevented masters from making their slaves work on Sunday—legislation that allowed the latter to attend worship services.[15] It would only be later in the eighteenth-century that slaveholders encouraged religious observances, in the hope of making the enslaved more docile and efficient labourers.

The first organized attempts to Christianize the African population in the American colonies began in earnest in 1701 by the SPG. Overseen by the bishop of London, the *Society* published tracts and sermons, and sent out missionaries and catechists to instruct the enslaved. Finding the time, permission, and money was always the greatest challenge facing the SPG. In 1710, a South Carolina missionary, Francis Le Jau, described his catechetical method:

---

14 Ibid.

15 Ibid, 100

> *Since it has pleased Almighty God to bless me*
> *with health I have upon Sundays after our divine*
> *service, invited the negroes and Indian slaves*
> *to stay for half an hour...we begin and end our*
> *particular assembly with the Collect Prevent us*
> *O Lord etc. I teach them the Creed, the Lord's*
> *Prayer, and the Commandments. I explain some*
> *portion of the catechism. I give them an entire*
> *liberty to ask questions. I endeavour to proportion*
> *my answers and all my instructions to their want*
> *and capacity.*[16]

Such instructions also required a formal statement from the SPG missionaries that baptism would not lead to freedom.[17] These missionary instructions did not lead to widespread conversions. Because the rote learning of scripture passages appealed to the intellect rather than the heart (and was simply parroting the missionary's instruction), such an approach had little impact on the enslaved community. By 1750 there were only a thousand baptized in the colony of Virginia; representing just one percent of the enslaved population.[18]

The greatest impact of the SPG was not conversion but literacy. The *Society* understood religious instruction to be a process of education. To that end—and

16 Albert J. Raboteau, op. cit., 115.

17 Alan Gallay, *Planters and Slaves in the Great Awakening* (Journal of Southern History, 1978), 24.

18 Guyraud S. Wilmore, *Black Religion and Black Radicalism* (New York: Doubleday & Co., 1972), 223.

in cooperation with a benevolent agency called the Associates of Dr Bray—several Negro schools were established in the colonies. Such educational endeavours proved more successful than religious catechisms. The first school opened on September 12, 1743, and lasted over twenty years, despite the fact that in 1740 the South Carolina Legislature passed a law prohibiting the teaching of the enslaved to read and write.[19] Because the school had already trained twenty-eight children and was currently instructing fifty-five more plus fifteen adults, it was allowed to continue.

But Africans were unwilling to accept form over substance. They saw the contradiction between the gospel of Jesus Christ and the gospel presented by the missionary and slave master. They displayed, therefore, a certain "contempt for book religion."[20] Africans were consciously (and perhaps unconsciously) aware that the knowledge of God acquired through the *Spirit* was far superior than bookish knowledge obtained via religious instruction. This is not to suggest that Africans had no regard for the Bible. In fact, just the opposite was true. Enslaved Africans had a high regard for the scriptures and listened very attentively when it was being read. Because of their amazing capacity to remember, Africans could recite whole chapters. Not being able to read, many believed that God revealed His *Word*

19 Albert J. Raboteau, op. cit., 116.

20 Gayraud S. Wilmore, op. cit., 9.

to them directly. It was believed "a converted heart and gifted tongue" was more important than theological training.[21] A missionary at Beaufort, South Carolina, heard a freed African woman state: "I don't know nothing! I can't read a word. But oh! I read Jesus in my heart, just as you read him in de book....I read and read him here in my heart, just as you read him in de Bible....I got Him! I hold him here all de time! He stays with me!"[22]

Several converted Africans related that they had come to know Bible verses because they had seen them in dreams. They had also come to understand that the God of the Bible was the God of the universe and superior to all other gods.[23] In Biblical stories and in the Prophets and the Psalms, Africans could see that the God of the Bible was just, and that rather than having to wait for a better life in the hereafter, they could hope for it in the here and now.

Africans were not content with mere religious instruction, but wanted an alternative experience. A direct experience of salvation was normative. "Conversion for slaves," writes Historian Albert J. Raboteau, "was a time of seeking, going apart to a quiet place, alone."[24] Going off to a quiet place and seeking are the prerequisites in the African Baptist oral tradition. David George, the founder of the ABC

---

21 Ibid, 133.
22 Albert J. Raboteau, op.cit., 242.
23 Ibid, 7.
24 Ibid, 73.

in Nova Scotia, was converted in South Carolina through the ministry of George Liele. In describing his conversion experience, George stated, "About this time more of my fellow-creatures began to seek the Lord."[25] In the African Baptist oral tradition, there may be several people seeking the Lord at the same time. The practice of 'going off to be alone' to seek the Lord was passed down over several generations, and may have, in fact, started in Africa. It was during this time that one would begin to experience dreams, visions, and voices.

Plantation missionaries were skeptical of experiences involving dreams. Nineteenth-century missionary, Charles Jones, states, "Negro converts were simply following a pattern of behaviour which had been handed down for generations, or which had begun in the wild fancy of some religious teacher among them."[26] Conversion for slaves could take place in any number of places and at any hour-- in the field, the woods, slave cabins, or at a camp meeting. John Jasper, a famous Negro preacher from Richmond, Virginia, was converted while working in a tobacco factory. In ungrammatical language, he recalls: "When de light broke, I was light as a feather; my feet was on de mount'n, salvation rol'd

---

25 John Rippon, *The Baptist Annual Register* (Southern Baptist Theological Seminary Library, Louisville Ky,1790-1793), 475.

26 Milton C. Sernett, op. cit., 85.

like a flood thru my soul, an I felt as if I could 'nock off de fact'ry roof wid my shouts."[27]

These revelatory experiences describe the inexpressible joy that is often felt at the moment of one's conversion: an experience that comes after several days (or sometimes weeks) of seeking. Not all conversion experiences are as intense or dramatic, but they do follow a certain pattern: solicitude, feelings of guilt, sadness, and images of dreams, visions, and voices of damnation, and salvation. Such dreams and images are often derived from Biblical themes. "The essential dynamic of the conversion", writes Raboteau, "is an inward, experiential realization of the doctrines of human depravity, divine sovereignty, and unconditional election made vividly apparent to the imagination and emotions."[28] A revivalist preacher named Pompey, recalls that his conversion was so radical "he doubted that he was the same person."[29] There is a popular spiritual sung in the African Baptist tradition called *"I'm Satisfied"*, that includes a line expressing this idea: "I looked at my hands, and my hands were new. I looked at my feet, and my feet were too." "...old things have passed away; behold, all things have become new."[30] True conversion, therefore, results in one experiencing a radical transformation.

---

27 Ibid, 84.

28 Albert J. Raboteau, op. cit., 268.

29 Ibid., 24.

30 2 Cor. 5:17.

The conversion process within the African Baptist oral tradition results in an intimate and secret knowledge of God. It is not the passive acceptance of believing what one has read or heard. Moreover, it is an affirmation of one's spiritual dignity accompanied by the ineffable joy of knowing one is saved! Such conversions revealed that God was not distant or indifferent to the daily sufferings of slave existence, but "...our refuge and strength, a very present help in trouble".[31]

The emphasis on having to withdraw to a place of solitude was not unique to the African Baptist experience. White southern Baptists (under the influence of the Great Awakening) also stressed the need to withdraw.[32] In Nova Scotia, the "going apart to a quiet place" would continue to be practised by the Preston-area churches well into the twentieth-century. Raboteau fails to mention, however, that the emphasis on *seeking* can be found both in the Old and New Testaments.[33] As shown in Matthew and Luke's Gospel, Jesus taught the need to seek.[34] "Truly you are God, who hide Himself," wrote the prophet Isaiah.[35] Because God is *hidden*, we must therefore seek after Him, in the hope of finding Him.

---

31 Ps. 46:1.
32 Matthew W. Cook, *The Impact of Revivalism on Baptist Faith and Practice*, 2009), 141.
33 Deut. 4:29, Jer. 29:12-13, Is. 55:6, Ps. 9:10, Pro. 1:28, Dan. 9:3, Matt. 6:33, 7:7, Lk. 11:9, Acts 17;27,Heb.11:6
34 Matt. 7:7, Lk. 11:9.

35 Is. 45:15.

The focus on an *inward* experience suggests that conversion is a subjective experience.[36] That is, it is of the heart, rather than of the head. Traditionally, when one becomes a member in the ABC, the candidate is not asked questions concerning the historic Christian doctrines. Instead, you are asked a series of questions relating to his/her experience, questions such as What do you put your strongest belief in? What you have heard? What you have seen? or what you have felt? The candidate then answers: "What I feel." Hence it is what one "feels" inwardly that determines whether one is saved. Another question asked: "Are you speaking to everyone?" In one particular church, if there were people in the community you were not speaking to, you were stopped in the middle of your testimony and required to go and make amends with that person. Another question is: "When will you need this faith most?" The answer is: "When I come down to die."

In the African Baptist oral tradition, the written *Word* (i.e., the Bible) must reach the heart as well as the head. This may help to explain why plantation missionaries were unsuccessful in their evangelistic efforts to convert large numbers of the enslaved. The old adage "Black people think with their hearts rather than their heads" may apply in this particular context.

---

36 Albert J. Raboteau, op. cit., 242.

Despite being considered illiterate by Western standards, Africans were not merely beasts-of-burden. They adapted Christianity to their own needs. They saw the advantages in showing an interest in religion.[37] Africans also saw the hypocrisy and disconnect between the White master's religion and his morality. They, therefore, "refused to be disciplined by the master's moral strictures."[38] African offences were often the result of their rejection of western standards of morality: a morality that was demanded of them but not reciprocated by the slaveholder, (e.g., slaveholders were often guilty of the very things they accused their slaves of). Yet slaves were not indifferent to pious masters and mistresses, or white Christians generally. William Wells Brown said of his master: "For his Christian zeal, I had the greatest respect, for I always regarded him as a truly pious and conscientious man."[39] David George relates in his narrative that his master, George Galphin, was "very good to him," describing him as a "great man." Solomon Northup, a free Black man from the North, who was sold into slavery, wrote of his master: "It is but simple justice to him when I say…there never was a more kind, noble, candid, Christian man than William Ford."[40]

---

37 Alan Gallay, op. cit., 35.

38 Gayraud S. Wilmore, op. cit., 10.

39 Milton C. Sernett, op. cit., 89.

40 Ibid., 89.

Many Africans accommodated themselves to orthodox Christianity as a means to an end, and therefore gave the appearance of conversion. It was advantageous to appear religious. Because Africans operated on a different system of values, their identities were always grounded in the slave community. That is to say, they did not inform on one another, as Whites did.[41] To use a contemporary expression, "they had each other's back." Engaging in petty theft and deception was not uncommon. The enslaved felt justified in stealing from their masters, because they were only taking what was rightfully theirs--what their labour had produced. "In order to keep body and soul together," writes Milton C.Sernett, "slaves often had to resort to behaviour which was...in violation of the customary standard of Christian morality."[42] Both Frederick Douglass and Booker T. Washington held that slavery had created its "own code of ethics." Washington's deeply pious mother was forced to steal eggs to feed her family. Washington wrote, "This would be classed as stealing, but deep down in my heart I can never decide that my mother, under such circumstances, was guilty of theft."[43] It was not that Christian slaves had no sense of right or wrong, but that their ultimate loyalty was to a higher morality than that practised by slaveholding Christians.

---

41 John B. Boles, *Master & Slaves in the House of the Lord* (Univ. Press of Kentucky, 1988) 79.

42 Milton C. Sernett, op. cit., 90.

43 Ibid, 91-92.

Missionaries and plantation preachers felt they had a moral obligation to convert the enslaved and told slave masters that they had a moral responsibility to do so. But Africans showed little interest in pro-slavery discourses and the moral admonitions to "obey your masters" with the hope of a reward in heaven. Often absent from church services, Africans were labelled by plantation preachers as "other-worldly" and "strangers to the house of the Lord."[44] Many slaveholders were not Christians, and were challenged by plantation preachers to accept the gospel into their own lives. Former slave, Charlie Van Dyke, complained,

> *Church was what they called it but all that preacher talked about was for us slaves to obey our masters and not to lie and steal. Nothing about Jesus was ever said and the overseer stood there to see the preacher talked as he wanted him to talk... even a black preacher would get up and repeat everything that the white preacher had said, because he was afraid to say anything different.*[45]

Though missionaries were granted permission by slaveholders to Christianize the enslaved, they did not achieve much success. This was especially the case among Africans born on the African continent, a fact noted in the SPG missionary reports of the

---

44 Erskine Clarke, *Westlin' Jacob: A Portrait of Religion in the Old South* (John Knox Press, Atlantic, 1941), 62.

45 Albert J. Raboteau, op. cit., 213-214.

era. The focus of missionary efforts, therefore, was on reaching the young rather than the adults. But it would be wrong to assume that the missionary efforts were without effect. "Whatever the lack of numerical effectiveness," writes Raboteau, "the religious instruction of slaves during the colonial period still had a significant impact on the lives of many slaves, missionaries, and masters."[46]

The African's religious experience has been dismissed by some as a mere "emotional catharsis" that allowed an outlet for the daily frustrations they were experiencing. However, it was more than this. It was a style of worship that had its roots in their African heritage. It revealed what it meant to be "African" in the New World. There was continuity between African and African-American forms of worship, explains Raboteau:

> *While the rhythms of the drums, so important in African and Latin American cults, were... forbidden to the enslaved in the United States, hand-clapping, foot-tapping, rhythmic preaching, hyperventilation antiphonal (call and response) singing, and dancing are styles of behaviour associated with possession both in Africa and in this country.*[47]

---

46 Ibid., 126.

47 Ibid., 65.

Former enslaved, Robert Anderson, describes the religious experience he witnessed as a youth during slavery:

> *The colored people...have a peculiar music of their own, which is largely a process of rhythm, rather than written music. Their music is largely, or was, a sort of rhythmical chant. It had to do with religion and the words adapted to their quaint melodies were of a religious nature. The stories of the Bible were placed into words that would fit the music already used by the colored people. While singing these songs, the singers and the entire congregation kept time to the music by the swaying of their bodies or the patting of the foot or hand. Practically all of their songs were accompanied by a motion of some kind. The weird and mysterious music of the religious ceremonies moved old and young alike in a frenzy of religious fervour. We also had religious dances that were expressions...of the fantastic, the mysterious that was felt in all our religious ceremonies.*[48]

But it was in the secrecy and seclusion of the hush arbors (hush harbours) "[that] slaves made Christianity truly their own".[49] It was in these secret meetings that Africans could freely express

---

48 Ibid.

49 Ibid., 212 Hush Arbors were secret meeting places where slaves would gather to worship in their own unique style. These gatherings usually took place at night.

themselves through song, dance, shouting, preaching, exhorting, and testimony. It was where the popular ring shout and the spiritual were born. It was in the hush arbors that the expression *old-time religion* was first coined, and where the *old time folk* gathered to sing the "old timely songs."[50] "I've got the old time religion in my heart", exclaimed one worshiper.[51]

Yet just as today, many African Baptists have not experienced the old time religion conversion. One former slave stated,

> *My religion means as much to me as anyone else, but I have not had...a chance to see any kind of funny forms or anything like that....This is my religion[:] 'Repent, believe, and be baptized, and you shall be saved.' This is my religion, and I believe it will take me to heaven...I have seen nothing nor heard nothing but only felt the spirit in my soul, and I believe that will save me when I come to die.*[52]

Spirituals were born out of the experience of suffering and human bondage. They were a blending of European and African cultures. Often taken from the Bible and combined with English hymns, spirituals told of the pain and pathos as well as the hopes and triumphs of slave existence. Replacing the names of African gods, spirituals were sung in praise

---

50 Albert J. Raboteau, op. cit., 220.

51 Ibid, 221.

52 Ibid., 270-71.

of the Christian God: the God of Abraham, Isaac, and Jacob. When asked where the lyrics came from, many would say "they came from God."

Benjamin Mays, former dean and president of Morehouse College, has described spirituals as a 'survival technique' that was created to help those enslaved endure their new reality in North America. He writes,

> *The creation of the spirituals was not an accident in Negro life. It was an imperative creation in order that the slave might adjust himself to the new conditions in the New World. They represent the soul-life of the people...these songs are the expressions of the restrictions and dominations which their creators experienced in the world about them.*[53]

One such spiritual was "*Go Down, Moses*":

> *When Israel was in Egypt's land, Let my people go, Oppressed so hard they could not stand, let my people go.*
> *Go down Moses, way down in Egypt's land, Tell old Pharaoh, let my people go!....*

Another spiritual was "*Oh Freedom*":

> *Oh freedom, Oh freedom, Oh freedom over me! And before I'll be a slave, I'll be buried in my grave,*

---

53 Benjamin Elijah Mays and Joseph William Nicholson, *The Negro's Church* (Russell & Russell, New York, 1933), 2.

And go home to my Lord and be free.
No more moaning, no more moaning,
No more moaning over me!
And before I'll be a slave, I'll be buried in
my grave,
And go home to my Lord and be free....

In many ABCs throughout Nova Scotia spirituals can still be heard. During Black Heritage Month (held every February), some churches hold *Negro Spiritual Night*. After the American Civil War, spirituals took written form. And many former slaves after the war felt there was no longer any need to sing spirituals. A new day had dawned!

For Africans enslaved in colonial America, Christianity reflected a different reality in a different milieu. From that matrix came something radically new.[54] Enslaved Africans came to believe that "the true substance of African Christianity was the authentic gospel of Jesus Christ, and was therefore superior to that practiced by whites."[55] Being already a religious people before arriving in the New World, one writer made the interesting observation that "the slave was lacking in every capacity but religion."[56] Historian, James W. St. G. Walker, made a similar comment in describing the Black Loyalists upon

---

54 Constance Bailey, *Give Me That Old-Time Religion, Reclaiming Slave Religion in the Future* (Master's Thesis, 2007), 34.

55 Donald G. Matthews, *Religion in the Old South* (Univ. of Chicago Press, Chicago, IL. 1979),190.

56 Ibid.,165.

their arrival in Nova Scotia. He states, "The foundation of their society, and its most distinctive trait, was religion." [57] God had "chosen the poor of this world" to be rich in faith.

Africans brought with them to the New World a worldview of a "sacred cosmos" over seen and sustained by a Supreme Deity."[58] In African spirituality, there is no rigid separation between the sacred and the secular, as understood in Western culture. The idea of a secular society versus a religious one does not exist, states Nova Scotian-born theologian, Peter J. Paris.[59] All reality was a reflection of God. This idea of reality being a reflection of God can also be seen in the thought of the Old Testament prophets.

African cosmology believed in a Superior Being pervading the cosmos was not an otherworldly concept. But rather, this Deity was understood as being involved in the practical and daily affairs of the community in a reciprocal relationship. In this covenant relationship the purpose and goal of the moral life "is the preservation and enhancement of the community."[60] It was also understood that violation of that covenant through acts of disobedience

---

57 James W. St. G. Walker, *The Black Loyalists, The Search for a Promise Land in Nova Scotia and Sierra Leone 1783-1870* (Dalhousie African Studies Series, Dalhousie University Press, 1975), 86.

58 Peter J. Paris, The Spirituality of African Peoples: The Search for a Moral Discourse (Fortress Press, Minneapolis, 1995), 34.

59 Ibid, 27

60 Ibid., 63.

could wreak havoc for the individual and his family as well as his community.[61]

The parallels between the God of the Bible and the gods of African spirituality notwithstanding, African spirituality tended to be backward-looking rather than forward-looking. It points to the past rather than to the future. Christianity on the other hand was progressive and forward-looking. There is the further belief that African ancestors still influenced the lives of loved ones even after they have died. Though life is seen as eternal, Africans did not share the Christian view of an after-life; or of a universal conception of humanity.[62] Because Christianity is linear and forward-looking, it gave the slave a reason to hope. This hope was expressed in the words of Nathaniel Paul, a former slave and pastor of the ABC in Albany, New York, when he stated, "We look forward with pleasing anticipation to that period when it shall no longer be said that in a land of freemen there are men in bondage."[63]

Paris sees many parallels between African-American religious practices and African sacred traditions. He argues that "the African-American experience cannot be fully appreciated without connecting with its African homeland."[64] Sociologist Franklin E. Frazier appears to take a different view,

61 Peter J. Paris, op. cit., 35.

62 Ibid., 52.

63 Henry J. Young, *Major Black Religious Leaders 1755-1940* (Abingdon Press, 1983), 21.

64 Peter J. Paris, op. cit., 20.

when he states, "It's impossible to establish any continuity between African religious practices and the Negro Church in the US."[65] What is true is that the vacuum left by the abandonment of the traditional gods of Africa was filled by Christianity, albeit a Christianity that was radically different from that practised by Europeans in the New World.

It was understood by the Western European nations from the very beginning of the Atlantic Slave Trade "that conversion of the slaves to Christianity was viewed...as a justification for enslavement of Africans,"[66] and that slavery, therefore, was seen as a "progressive institution ordained by God to Christianize Africans." [67] This belief was reinforced by citing the Biblical account of Noah's curse on his grandson, Canaan, the son of Ham, found in Genesis chapter nine. Canaan was indirectly blamed for the actions of his father. The curse of Ham, therefore, would be one of subjugation and human servitude. Ham was, it was believed, the original ancestor of Africans----a belief that is still held today by some. A further justification for slavery was that Africans would benefit from the exposure of Western civilization. Europeans arrogantly saw themselves as "the personification of Christian civilization."[68]

---

65 Franklin Frazier, *The Negro Church in America* (Schocken Books, New York, 1963), 13.

66 Albert J. Raboteau, op. cit., 96

67 John B. Boles, Masters and Slaves in the House of the Lord (University Press of Kentucky, 1988), 6.

68 Donald G. Matthews, op. cit., 145.

Africans, however, interpreted scripture as it related to their enslavement. They identified their enslavement with the Biblical Israelites, and comparing it to Israel's enslavement in Egypt.[69] Consequently, certain Old Testament themes and characters became an integral part of African Christianity. Many of the slave population further believed that slavery was the result of irreverent acts and disobedience to God.[70] Enslaved Christians, on the other hand, interpreted their suffering as sharing in the sufferings of Christ. Historian Arnold Toynbee, would later write, "The Negro rediscovered during slavery the original meaning of Christianity: that Jesus was a prophet who came into the world not to confirm the mighty in their seats but to exalt the humble and meek."[71] And just as God had delivered the Children of Israel from Egyptian bondage, He would liberate the enslaved African in the New World.

Liberty for those formerly enslaved at least within the British Empire did finally come with the passage of the *Slavery Abolition Act,* which was given Royal Assent on August 28, 1833. This Act would officially come into force on August 1, 1834.

---

69 Cf. Susel Perez's essay *Slavery in the Western Hemisphere*: (Slave Religion, 2010), 2.

70 Lawrence W. Levine, *Black Culture and Black Consciousness: Afro-American Folk Thought from Slavery to Freedom* (New York, Oxford University Press, 1977), 34.

71 Arnold J. Toynbee, *A study of History* (Oxford Univ. Press, 1947), 129.

Chapter Two

African Baptists and the Great Awakening

In tracing the roots of the oral tradition and history of the ABC, it would not be until the first Great Awakening[72] that the effort to evangelize the enslaved community would be attempted. Beginning in 1734, America witnessed a spiritual revival and religious awakening that would forever change the theological discourse and meaning of salvation in American Christianity.

The Great Awakening—which would soon evolve into a movement—was first initiated by a small group of devoted evangelical preachers. Their simple but emotional message was a radical departure from the missionary efforts and the more formal, academic

---

72 The Great Awakening was a religious and social revival that began in the 1730s and 40s. It represented a decisive break with organized religion and the established church. The period was the beginning of the Age of the Enlightenment.

and sedate sermons offered by organized religion. Rather, it was based on the Protestant Reformation principle of the "Priesthood of All Believers," that is to say, everyone was an heir to the gospel of Christ, and therefore responsible for the salvation of others' souls. Or, as one southern pastor stated, "A free salvation to all men thro' the blood of the Lamb."[73] (More will be said about the central role of the blood in the next chapter).

Evangelical preachers of the Awakening such as Jonathan Edwards, George Whitefield, and Samuel Davies preached an Arminian doctrine that "God would save all who believed in Him...that salvation was there for all to take hold of if they would."[74] Theirs was a fervent and rousing message that was aimed at the heart rather than the head and intellect. This radical message of religious regeneration called for an "inward" conversion that stressed "conviction, repentance, regeneration and the drama of sin and salvation."[75] Its overarching theme was that all humankind was sinful and must seek redemption and God's forgiveness.

Perhaps even more significant was the emphasis the Great Awakening placed on spiritual equality, which appealed to both Blacks and Whites alike. The Great Awakening was both a spiritual and humanitarian phenomenon motivated by democratic

---

73 Albert J. Raboteau, op. cit., 132.

74 Ibid.

75 Ibid.

ideals. Such ideals included evangelical activism, humanitarianism, pastoral care, and a condemnation of unregenerate clergy.[76] At revival gatherings the enslaved were accorded equal status as full human beings. Evangelism provided a refuge and style of worship that the African community had not previously experienced in North America. Evangelicals therefore became a threat and challenge to the institution of slavery.[77]

The four denominations most impacted by the Awakening were the Baptists, Methodists, Congregationalist, and the Presbyterians. The Baptist and Methodist denominations were folk churches that appealed to the poor and marginalized of all races. Their emotional and lively message found a receptive audience among the poor and downtrodden, enslaved and free, Black and White. The evangelistic message of the Awakening gave expression to the daily agony, brutality, and dehumanization of slave existence. This resulted in many of the enslaved joining the Baptist and Methodist churches in massive numbers. One of the reasons for this huge influx and appeal was that the Baptists and Methodists were opposed to slavery, and most did not own slaves. In 1789, the Baptist General Committee of Virginia passed the following resolution:

---

76 Alan Gallay, op.cit., 21.

77 Ibid, p. 24.

> *Resolved that slavery is a violent deprivation of*
> *the rights of nature, and inconsistent with a repub-*
> *lican government; and we, therefore recommend it*
> *to our brethren, to make use of every legal measure*
> *to extirpate this horrid evil from the land and pray*
> *Almighty God that our honourable legislature may*
> *have it in their power to proclaim the great Jubilee*
> *consistent with the principles of good policy.*[78]

Though stopping short of calling for the total dismantling of the slave system, the Methodists expressed their official opposition to slavery in its *General Rules* developed by Charles Wesley in 1743. These were reaffirmed again at its 1784 Christmas Conference in Philadelphia.[79] Methodists also refused membership to those who owned slaves.

Secondly, the Baptists and Methodists were inclusive and democratic, which allowed for African participation in their services. Baptists were among the first to license and allow Africans to preach; the only qualification was feeling "the call."

Thirdly, the emphasis of these denominations was on conversion and feeling; rather than catechism and religious instruction, which had been the rule by established denominations. Baptists were anti-establishment; they criticized organized

---

78 Mechhal Sobel, *Trabelin' On: The Slave Journey To An Afro-Baptist Faith* (Greenwood Press, Westport, Conn, 1979), 86.

79 C. Eric Lincoln and Lawrence H. Mamiya, *The Black Church in the African American Experience* (Duke University Press, Durham and London, 1990), 50.

religion and established authority. Because of this, in the South they were whipped, jailed, and run out of communities.[80]

In these southern interracial Baptist churches the enslaved were not only free to sing, shout, testify and feel, they had their dignity as human beings affirmed. They addressed each other as sister and brother, and received communion along with their White counterparts. Africans also served as deacons, elders, and exhorters who preached to White congregations. Some of the pioneering Black preachers to emerge during this period were men such as George Liele, David George, Jupiter Hammon, and Andrew Bryan.[81]

Despite still being enslaved, Africans enjoyed a spiritual freedom that was unprecedented. The "Spirit of God" in its true expression is one of "creative unity": one that transcends the barriers of colour and culture, race and religion, social class, and one's economic status. During this time of integrated worship, White pastors could be found pastoring all-African churches. Robert Ryland was the White pastor of the First African Baptist Church of Richmond for twenty-five years.[82]

The impact of the Awakening had a reciprocal effect on both African and White Baptists. What

---

80 Mechal Sobel, op. cit., 85.

81 Thomas, Thomas, Duncan, Ray, Jr., and Westfield, *Black Church Studies* (Abingdon Press, Nashville, 2007), 7.

82 C. Eric Lincoln and Lawrence H. Mamiya, op.cit, 24.

had previously been a racist and paternalistic relationship was transformed into one of mutual respect and religious harmony. Historian Mechal Sobel described the emotional impact of the revivals on both Africans and White Baptists in these words: "For the first time [they] saw whites responding to a religious demand with the totality of their being and participating in religious trances, shouts, moaning and rebirth."[83] Sobel goes on to explain in great detail the similarity in the religious conversions between Africans and Whites, including the role and importance of dreams. "Both recount the worthlessness of the sinner" writes Sobel, "his sense of eternal damnation, his sudden salvation, and...joy at having experience with God and the assurance of God in his soul."[84]

While pointing out the similarities in the conversion experiences between African and White Baptists (e.g., state of sinfulness, condemnation, sudden conversion, and regeneration), Sobel also points out the dissimilarities. African cultural, religious expressions began to be singled out as particularly ecstatic by White Baptists, "signifying consciousness of a difference."[85] By 1840 a Reverend Hosea Holcombe made the observation that "a great number of those (Negroes) who unite with our churches, express

---

83 Mechal Sobel, op. cit., 98.

84 Ibid, 107.

85 Ibid.

themselves in a very visionary manner, implying a qualitative difference from white conversions."[86]

Moreover, as White Baptists moved from being a sect to a denomination and therefore more organized and institutionalized, experiential religion began to decline. This transition from sect to denomination over time meant less emphasis on dreams and visionary experiences. Sobel gives particular attention to the conversion experiences of George Liele and David George, and their far-reaching effects. It is here that we gain greater insight into the origins of the African Baptist oral tradition. In describing the conversions of Liele and George, Sobel writes, "George Liele and David George were reborn in a black Baptist faith through which they gained a new sense of their selves, a new individuality, and a new purpose....They began new lives as a result... of the coherence they achieved in the black Baptist Sacred Cosmos."[87]

Sobel describes this "black Baptist Sacred Cosmos" not as an impersonal cosmos, but one in which [Africans] were in dialogue.[88] The African Baptist oral tradition affirms the belief in a "personal

---

86 Ibid.

87 Mechal Sobel, op.cit., 107.

88 We saw in the previous chapter that in African cosmology there is the belief in the sacredness of the cosmos, and that it is governed by a Supreme Being who has a reciprocal relationship to the community. It will further be shown in this chapter that Sobel describes the members at the Silver Bluff Church as "seekers," where George was a member, and Liele helped found.

God", that can be known and experienced. Such a worldview was most appealing to African Baptists because it was an Afro-Baptist cosmos. The visionary experiences of African Baptists became more unique and pronounced as White Baptist became more conformist and less concerned with spiritual journeys.[89]

Despite Sobel's excellent and exhaustive analysis of the Afro-Baptist experience, there is a conspicuous absence of any mention of the blood, and its role in the conversion experience[90]. For seekers in the Baptist tradition seeing and experiencing the blood of Christ was *the* determining factor in one's salvation. Fundamental to that tradition is the belief that one is never considered *saved* until you have experienced the cleansing power of the blood. It is witnessing to the blood that the candidate is examined, tested, and tried. This aspect of the African Baptist oral tradition it represents one of the great hidden mysteries of the faith, and stands at the centre of that tradition. And yet this aspect of the Christian faith has been greatly neglected in much contemporary Christian thought. (As William Cowper's 1772 hymn states, there is still "a fountain filled with blood drawing from Immanuel's vein!")

---

89 Mechal Sobel, op.cit., 108.

90 A prevalent belief in Christianity that is expressed in many church hymns is that Christ's shed blood was necessary for our salvation; and that without such a sacrificial atonement there is no forgiveness of sin.

Africans were attracted to Christianity because of the parallels found between Christianity and traditional African religions. For example, most West African religions consisted of a tripartite hierarchy of deities and the belief in a Supreme Being. For Africans converting to Christianity, this 'hierarchy of deities' was expressed in the Trinity of the Father, Son, and Holy Spirit. Spirit possession was another characteristic of African religion, which for Christianity was a sign of receiving the Holy Spirit. The rite of water baptism bore similarities to that of the water cults of West Africa. Therefore, writes Raboteau, "there were enough similarities to make it possible for slaves to find some common ground between the beliefs of their ancestors and those of white Christians."[91]

Though other mainline denominations were influenced by the evangelistic preaching of the Awakening (Anglicans, Puritans, Presbyterians) it was the Baptists and Methodists who would come to dominate the lives of the African community. This was especially true in the southern, rural colonies—South Carolina, Georgia, Virginia—where most African Baptists and Methodists were concentrated. While the African Methodists are credited with founding the first separate denomination, the African Baptists founded the earliest Black churches,

---

91 Albert J Raboteau, op. cit., 127.

and have the largest number of members of any other denomination.[92]

Despite the initial evangelistic impact on the enslaved community, it did not always last. Not all slaves accepted the theology and practices of the Great Awakening. By the time of the American Revolution in 1776, only about two percent of America's enslaved population were professing Christians.[93] Africans would join the church during revivals and camp meetings, but then would lose interest after the revival. This phenomenon of making an emotional response to the gospel "in the moment" and then backsliding can still be seen today. One may be convicted but not necessarily converted. Sudden bursts of emotion are not synonymous with the inner workings of the Holy Spirit. They are not one and the same.

Further, White evangelists continued to insist that as good Christians, and in obedience to God, the enslaved community was still expected to "obey their masters." Evangelical faith was not synonymous with freedom; slaves continued to experience discrimination in bi-racial churches. In 1786, southern churches began to physically separate their members by race. This racial distinction resulted in segregated seating. Sobel writes, "An important result of the

---

92 C. Eric Lincoln and Lawrence H. Mamiya, op. cit., 46. Whether African Baptists can claim today in 2024 to have the largest number of members of any denomination such data isn't available.

93 www.pbs.org/thisfarbyfaith, p 6

new conformist tendencies in Baptist circles was the growing desire of whites in mixed churches to separate from their black brothers and sisters."[94]

With greater numbers of Africans joining the Baptist church, it was only a matter of time before all-Black Baptist churches were established. In 1755, Shubal Stearns, a White itinerant preacher from Connecticut, established the first all-black Baptist congregation.[95] Stearns would organize several New Light-Baptist churches in the South.[96] In 1758 another ABC was formally constituted on the plantation of William Byrd, in Mecklenburg, Virginia. All-Black Baptist churches were founded on several plantations throughout the South in the eighteenth-century.

The earliest southern churches were established in Virginia (1758), South Carolina (1773), and Georgia (1777).[97] The church in South Carolina, called the Silver Bluff Baptist Church, was organized by a White itinerant preacher and evangelist

---

94 Mechal Sobel, op. cit., 190.

95 Ibid., 102.

96 New Light Baptists resulted from a split within the Baptist movement during the first Great Awakening. They were also known as *Separate Baptists*, (distinct from Old Light, Regular Baptists) who practised a rigorous Calvinism and were intensely emotional in their revival endeavors. Henry Alline, the Congregationalist preacher from Rhode Island, established several *New Light* chapels in Nova Scotia in the eighteenth-century, which eventually evolved into present-day White Baptist congregations.

97 www.pbs.org/This Far by Faith p.6

from Connecticut, named Wait (Weight or Wight) Palmer, and an enslaved lay preacher named George Liele, between 1773-1775.[98] Palmer was a product of the first Awakening and was ordained in 1743. He established the first Baptist church in North Stonington, Connecticut. An itinerate preacher in the southern colonies, Palmer was responsible for establishing several revivalist New Light Baptist churches.[99] Silver Bluff would serve as the mother church for Baptist missions in the South. It was also the church where David George was a member; in time, he would become the church's pastor.

As independent ABC multiplied, others were established in cities such as Williamsburg, Richmond, and Petersburg, Virginia, which had large African populations, including many emancipated Africans. The fact that Black independent churches were self-governing posed a serious threat to both civil and ecclesiastical authorities. Such religious autonomy was seen as granting too much freedom and independence to a people who were still (at least legally) not free. Many whites doubted whether Africans were even capable of managing their own institutions. This criticism led to a complaint in the *South Carolina Gazette* on April 24, 1742, that: "Instead of teaching them the *Principles*

---

98 Grant Gordon, *From Slavery to Freedom: The Life of David George, Pioneer Black Baptist Minister* (Lancelot Press Ltd., Hantsport, NS, 1992), 27.

99 Ibid, 25.

of Christianity, irresponsible preachers were filling their heads with a parcel of "Cant-Phrases, Trances, Dreams, Visions and Revelations."[100] These and other complaints against all-Black churches led local authorities and plantation owners to impose certain restrictions. Written permission would now be required for those enslaved to travel to other plantations for worship. Many African Baptists would only be allowed to attend the churches of their masters or African churches pastored by white clergy. Under no circumstances were ABCs permitted to form an all-African Baptist association.[101] As greater restrictions on ABCs increased, "independent" became a misnomer. The control of Black churches in the South continued into the nineteenth-century:

> *...In the South a large congregation of colored people could lay no claim to sovereignty apart from white people. This point is illustrated in the first African Baptist Church, Savannah, whose membership of seven hundred was divided into three churches by the Savannah Association in 1802. Only after emancipation can complete autonomy is called a distinguishing mark of a Negro Baptist Church.*[102]

Frustrated with the shortcomings and discrimination encountered in bi-racial churches, African

---

100 Mechal Sobel, op.cit., 102.
101 C. Eric Lincoln and Lawrence H. Mamiya, op.cit., 25.
102 Ibid

Baptists responded to such treatment by establishing their own churches. Spiritual equality, they discovered, did not imply freedom from racial discrimination even within the "Body of Christ." James Walker, in describing the Baptist congregations established by David George in Nova Scotia, and the latter's emphasis on freedom, writes, "A people desiring freedom, equality, local democracy, and popular participation in the affairs of their church found those things in the Baptist chapels inspired by David George."[103] The theme of "freedom" has characterized much of African-American Christianity throughout its history.

But separation from White congregations did not result in African Baptists abandoning Protestant Evangelicalism, Baptist doctrine, or denominational polity. Booker T. Washington, writing in the nineteenth-century, described the connection between Black and White Christians and Protestant orthodoxy: "The two were as distinct socially", he wrote, "as the five fingers of the hand, but they were one like the hand itself in sharing the Evangelical heritage."[104] Such separation was not only a desire to be free from White domination and discrimination, but also a desire for "independent cultural expression, and a defence against racism."[105]

---

103 James W. St. G. Walker, op.cit., 76.

104 Milton C. Sernett, op. cit., 18.

105 Eugene Genovese, *Roll, Jordan, Roll: The World the Slave Made* (New York: Pantheon, 1974), 235.

The African Baptist denominations that grew out of the Great Awakening of the eighteenth-century were of three types: Plantation Baptists, Balcony Baptists, and Invisible Baptists. It was the "Invisible Baptists" from which the oral tradition would develop. Their spiritual legacy is the focus of this project. We shall discuss each of these three Baptist groups in turn.

Plantation Baptists were those who worshipped on the plantation of their masters. These Baptists were always supervised by an overseer or their master. White presence ensured that nothing would be done or preached that would pose a threat to the planters or the plantation system. Outnumbered by their enslaved population, Whites lived in perpetual fear of rebellions and insurrections whenever slaves gathered in large numbers. The Plantation Baptist preacher was usually hired by the master and was sometimes the master himself. Even when the preacher was a fellow African, the message was the same: a distorted presentation of the Christian faith. Certain Biblical text were emphasized, (e.g., Paul's Epistle to Philemon), and similar passages that stressed "the duties of servant to master." Often out of disgust slaves would hold their own services once the plantation service ended.[106]

Balcony Baptists were those who attended church along with their master and his family. They were

---

106 Albert J. Raboteau, op. cit., 213.

confined to the balcony, the gallery, or the back of the church. If there was not sufficient room in the sanctuary, slaves would be forced to sit next to a window outside of the church. Segregating slaves during worship was not unique to the South; it was widespread in both the North and South during the colonial era. "Blacks found themselves", writes Henry J. Young, "segregated in and alienated from the same churches that they contributed to financially and physically in their construction."[107]

As the name suggests, Invisible Baptists (also called the Invisible Institution) were a secret, clandestine fellowship that met informally at night in some designated location. It is where the "old-time folk" would gather, hence the name old-time religion. These nocturnal gatherings—which usually took place after midnight and lasted for hours—were also called by other names: brush arbors, praying ground, or out on the branches.[108] The Negro spiritual, Steal Away (now known universally) began as a secret code indicating that a clandestine meeting was to take place.

Brush Arbor meetings often required travelling several miles through wooded areas and thickets to get to these secret locations. They might be held in a gully, ravine, or open field. Slaves would go to

107 Henry J. Young, *Major Black Religious Leaders 1755-1940* (Abingdon Press, Nashville, Tennessee, 1983), 28.

108 Dwight H. Hopkins, *Down, Up and Over: Slave Religion and Black Theology* (Fortress Press, Minneapolis, 2000), 117-18.

great lengths to stifle the sound of their worship. One method of preventing the sound from travelling was by turning pots upside down, or filling vessels with water. Another was soaking blankets and rags in water and hanging them around the perimeter of the worship site. "It was in the secrecy of the quarters and the seclusion of the brush arbors", writes Raboteau, that "the slaves made Christianity truly their own."[109]

These nightly gatherings put those in attendance at great risk because they could bring down the wrath of the night patrols—whose role it was to spy on the nightly activities within the slave quarters. If caught at such services, slaves could be severely punished. Moses Grandy reported that his brother-in-law, Isaac, a slave preacher, was flogged for speaking at a secret meeting. Those in attendance were also whipped and "forced to tell who else was there."[110] Suffering indignities for the sake of the gospel was a frequent occurrence. Andrew Bryan, a former slave and the first pastor of the Savannah African Baptist Church, and his brother Sampson, a deacon, were arrested, publicly whipped and imprisoned. Knowledge of such treatment reveals that the African Baptist oral tradition was born out of the crucible of suffering and sorrow: that Africans did not only suffer as a result of their enslavement, but equally as Christians.

---

109 Albert J. Raboteau, op. cit, 212.

110 Ibid., 214.

These secret meetings would sometimes take place in the slave quarters. Masters, under the cloak of darkness, would go to the quarters hoping to catch slaves in the act of worship. Africans worshipping at night without White supervision was considered a major threat to the stability of plantation life. Slaveholders understood that secret, religious meetings could also serve as planning sessions for slave insurrections and rebellions[111]. In 1800 South Carolina banned all religious gatherings between sunset and sunrise. Yet enslaved Africans were still willing to take the risk to be together to encourage each other in the faith.

In addition to the singing, exhorting, preaching, and handclapping that were an integral part of Invisible Baptist worship, testimonies were heard of what the Lord was doing, "how they were feeling, and the state of their minds."[112] Today candidates for baptism are still asked similar questions when coming before the membership to tell their experience. Free from White supervision, slaves could be themselves and worship without restrictions. It was in these secluded, sacred spaces that the spirituals and "ring-shout" became popular—which continue to this day. A former slave shared his experience of these secluded meetings:

> *Meetings back then meant more than they do now. Then everybody's heart was in tune, and when*

---

111 Guyraud S. Wilmore, op. cit., 46.

112 Quoted from *Peter Randolph's Autobiography*, 1893, 202.

they called upon God they made heaven ring...
they would steal off to the fields and in the thickets
and there, with heads together around a kettle
to deaden the sound, they called on God out of
heavy hearts.[113]

Fervent prayers to God were not confined to present problems and situations; they also included prayers to be free in the future—and not only for the enslaved themselves, but for their children and future generations. One enslaved, Alice Sewell, vividly recalled praying for a better future for her offspring: "We come from four or five miles to pray together to God dat if we don't live to see it, to please let our children live to see a better day and be free...."[114] Such petitions show the progressive, forward-thinking nature of these nightly gatherings.

To say that 'everyone's heart was in tune' meant that those who came together were bound by a common, religious experience.[115] Where a common, shared experience is lacking, there can be no true *Koinonia* (i.e. fellowship). It expresses the true character of the African Baptist oral tradition. It was not merely the singing, shouting, exhorting, praying and preaching, that motivated the Invisible Baptists, but rather all having the same experience.

---

113 Dwight N. Hopkins, op .cit., 137.
114 Ibid., 139.

115 All have the same common experience is one of the unique aspects of the old time religion.

Invisible Baptists were both visible and invisible. That is to say, those participating in the invisible church were also members of the official institutional church. "The religion of the slaves," states Raboteau, "was institutional and non-institutional, visible and invisible, formally organized and spontaneously adapted."[116] The invisible church was hidden within the visible, organized church. (This phenomenon can be seen today in some Baptist churches where some members may not have had a traditional experience, while other members may have). As mentioned earlier, the invisible church was characterized by secrecy; and one of those secrets was the telling of one's *experience*.

An example of one such Baptist church (which has already been mentioned) that was both visible and invisible was the one organized at Silver Bluff, South Carolina by Pastor Palmer. Silver Bluff was a trading post and stood at the crossroads of economic activity. It was located on the South Carolina side of the Savannah River, twelve miles from Augusta, Georgia. The Silver Bluff church met in the mill located on the plantation owned by George Galphin, who was the master of David George. The church at Silver Bluff is reputed to be the first and oldest of all-Black Baptist congregations in North America.[117] George was one of its founding members.

---

116 Albert J. Raboteau, op. cit., 212.

117 Grant Gordon, op. cit., 27.

David George relates in his 1793 narrative that Pastor Palmer "organized them into a church and administered the Lord's Supper." He further stated that up until 1770 when he married his wife Phyllis, he lived "a very bad life and had no thoughts about my soul."[118] George recounted,

> *A man of my color, named Cyrus, told me one day in the woods that if I lived so I should never see the face of God in glory. This was the first thing that disturbed me and gave me much concern. I thought then that I must be saved by prayer. I used to say the Lord's Prayer...but I feared that I grew worse....*[119]

George now felt the promptings of the Spirit but could not find deliverance. He was convicted but had yet to experience conversion. His state continued to worsen to the point where he could not serve his master. He wrote, "I felt my own plaque; and was so overcome that I could not wait on my master. I told him I was ill. I felt myself at the disposal of Sovereign mercy."[120] What is revealing in this statement is the futility in attempting to effect one's own salvation.

George's experience is not unlike that of other spiritually exceptional individuals who had undergone a radical religious conversion (e.g., Luther, Fox,

---

118 John Rippon, *The Baptist Annual Register* (Southern Baptist Theological Seminary Library), Louisville Ky., 1790), 474.
119 Ibid., p 475.

120 Ibid

and Tolstoy) whose conversions were preceded by deep despair and anguish of soul. George Fox, the founder of the Quakers, wrote,

> *I fasted much, walked abroad in solitary places many days...and frequently in the night walked mournfully about by myself; for I was a man of sorrows in the time of the first workings of the Lord in me.*[121]

The Bible describes the death of the old self and the birth of the new this way: "...unless a corn of wheat falls into the ground and dies, it remains alone; but if it dies, it produces much grain."[122] It is in the putting to death of the old self that a "new creation" [123] is realized. George would go on to produce a great harvest!

George explained that more of his fellow-creatures "began to seek the Lord." The practice of several people seeking the Lord at the same time was not uncommon in the Preston-area churches during the time of revivals.[124] George did not, however, explain what "seeking the Lord" entailed. Sobel seems to suggest that seeking may have been unique to the Silver Bluff congregation. She states, "A Brother

---

121 William James, *The Varieties of Religious Experience* (New American Library of World Literature. Inc., 1958), 262.
122 Jn. 12:24.
123 2 Cor. 5:17.

124 The time of revivals was an annual event coinciding with the "Season of Lent" and lasting for two weeks.

Palmer [perhaps Reverend Wait Palmer], a powerful preacher, who frequently preached to the Silver Bluff "seekers."[125] It may be concluded from this statement that the practice of "seeking" was also a part of the Baptist tradition practised by the first African Baptist Church founded by David George in Nova Scotia, and that this practice continued well into the twentieth-century. While still enslaved, George and seven others (including his wife) experienced conversion and "found the great blessing and mercy from the Lord."[126]

George was 50 years old at the time of his conversion. He later stated that Palmer appointed a Saturday evening to "hear what the Lord had done." Being convinced that the eight candidates were converted, Pastor Palmer baptized them in a nearby stream. The expression "'hearing what the Lord had done'" will be a constant theme throughout George's ministry. It suggests that 'what God has done' was the workings of the Holy Spirit and not of human effort. It is what God Himself has done! How widespread the practice of hearing conversion experiences was among African Baptists in the antebellum South cannot be determined. George would, however, continue this tradition upon his arrival in Nova Scotia.

Following his conversion, George sensed the call of God on his life, and began to "exhort in the church and sing hymns." Recognizing his

---

125 Mechal Sobel, op.cit., 106.

126 John Rippon, op. cit., 475.

potential for leadership, George's church "advised with Brother Palmer about my speaking to them, and keeping them together."[127] Feeling unworthy and unequal to the task, George declined the offer. Pastor Palmer admonished George for refusing to accept the church's request, by saying, "Take care that you don't offend the Lord."[128] George's reluctance to accept the challenge of leadership is not uncommon among those when the "call of God" is upon one's life. Despite his sense of inadequacy, but feeling that "Palmer knew best," George accepted the offer and was made an elder under Palmer's guidance.

One of George's inadequacies—and like most of those enslaved—was his illiteracy. He related that he first attempted to teach himself to read by getting a spelling book. He wrote,

> *Master was a great man, he kept a school-master to teach the white children to read. I used to go to the little children to teach me a, b, c. They would give me a lesson, which I tried to learn, and then I would go to them again, and ask them if I was right? The reading so ran in my mind that I think I learned in my sleep…as when I was awake. And I can now read the Bible, so that what I have in my heart, I can see again in the Scriptures.*[129]

---

127 John Rippon, op. cit., 476

128 Ibid.

129 Ibid.

George would not only learn to read, but as he grew in grace, he would also learn to write.

With the approaching of the American War of Independence in 1775, itinerant preachers could no longer travel freely among the enslaved population. Slaveholders feared that Black preachers would share too much knowledge about freedom to their enslaved congregations. This resulted in George becoming the sole pastor of the Silver Bluff Baptist Church. With the capture of Savannah by the British, George's master (being a patriot) was forced to flee. This left George and his church (now consisting of more than thirty members) to "fend for themselves." Unable to keep his church intact, George's congregants were forced to disperse. George, along with his family and fifty fellow-slaves, travelled to a place called Ebenezer, some twenty miles from Savannah, where they came under the protection of the British.

From Ebenezer George was sent to Savage's plantation, near Savannah. Grant Gordon reports that upon George's arrival at Savage's plantation, he was accused of "planning to carry the Black people back again to their slavery."[130] Obviously there was some misunderstanding regarding this false charge against George; and Gordon did not explain its origins. George was put into prison, where he languished for a month. The accusation against him was found to be groundless. He was soon released by the British and

---

130 Grant Gordon, op. cit., 31.

stayed for some time in Savannah in a place called Yamacraw. It was in Yamacraw that George reunited with his childhood friend and fellow pastor, George Liele. Liele had also been an influence in George's conversion at Silver Bluff and had founded a Baptist church at Yamacraw in December, 1777.

George and the members from Silver Bluff joined the church at Yamacraw, where Liele served as pastor. George made his home in Savannah for two years, before moving on to Charleston, where he was given legal protection by the British for the rest of his stay in the city. When bound for Nova Scotia he carried with him two official documents certifying his legal status as a British subject. The two documents read: (1) "Permit the bearer {David George} to pass and repass about his lawful business unmolested," (2), "The within mentioned David George has a wife named Phyllis and three children (who are also free) Jesse, David, and Ginny, who are all recommended to the protection of his Majesty's Subjects."[131]

George and his family sailed to Nova Scotia from Charleston in the fall of 1782. He wrote, "When the English were going to evacuate Charleston, they advised me to go to Halifax, Nova Scotia."[132] Both the 56 Blacks and 500 Whites on George's evacuation vessel were given free passage in consequence of their loyalty to the Crown.

---

131 Ibid., 35.

132 John Rippon, op. cit., 477.

Guided by God's hidden providence, David George's departure from the newly founded American Republic brought to a close his life of human bondage. Now a free man and British subject, George would begin anew his ministry where he would sing the Songs of Zion in a New Land. He would establish the first African Baptist Church in Canada, the second Baptist church in Nova Scotia, and the first in the Loyalist settlement of Shelburne.

Chapter Three

David George and the Black Loyalists

This survey began with looking at the seventeenth-century and the transatlantic slave trade, and the first organized missionary attempt to introduce Christianity to the enslaved African population. These efforts would eventually culminate in the first Great Awakening. From this great awakening would emerge the African Baptist Church movement. This chapter will examine David George's ministry, his theology, and the ABCs he established in Nova Scotia. It will also look at the African Baptist conversion experience.

At the end of the American War of Independence in 1783, some 30,000 Americans arrived in Nova Scotia as British Loyalists; most of these Loyalists were Anglican. Among this number were 3,500 former enslaved Africans, who had been offered their freedom and land in exchange for their loyalty to the British Crown. Most of the emancipated slaves were either Baptists or Methodists. There were also small groups of Anglicans, Roman Catholics, Presbyterians, and Huntingdonians (a splinter group of the Methodists) as well as some who were of no religious persuasion.

Historically known as the Black Loyalists, many were skilled in certain occupations such as blacksmiths, coopers, tailors, shoemakers, carpenters. Some were cooks, bakers, and waiters.[133] Most of these recently freed Africans identified with the dominant culture and religion of the day and many were baptized as Anglicans.[134] Because the Church of England had the necessary resources and influence, it was usually the first denomination to do mission work in the various segregated Black communities throughout Nova Scotia. In the first year of the Loyalists' arrival, hundreds of Blacks were baptized—both adults and children. Rather than becoming Anglicans out of a spiritual conviction, these converts believed that baptism into the Church of England would ensure their freedom and equality in a society dominated by the Anglican Establishment. In his recent book, titled *Black Loyalists in New Brunswick*, Nova Scotian

---

133 Bridglal Pachai, *Beneath the Clouds of the Promise Land: The Survival of Nova Scotia's Blacks*, vol 1, (McCurdy Printing & Typesetting Limited), 1987, 43.

134 James W. St. G. Walker, op. cit., 66-67. The Church of England established a presence in Nova Scotia as early as 1749, with the founding of Halifax. It was therefore the most powerful and influential of the established churches.

educator and historian, Stephen Davidson, describes the importance for Black Loyalists to be baptized as Anglicans. He writes, "Baptism in the Anglican Church had a special significance for Black Loyalists: according to the church's theology, baptized persons were 'all one and equal in Christ'. Here they were equal with white believers."[135]

While Anglican theology might have stated in principle the *equality of all believers*, it was not the reality. Davidson continues: "But even within the Anglican Communion, Blacks were not treated as fellow congregants. Typically, they sat in pews at the back of churches alongside the slaves of white parishioners."[136]

The practice of segregating Blacks was similar to that found in the Balcony Baptist churches of the antebellum American South. A special gallery was built at St Paul's Anglican Church in Halifax, in 1784, where Blacks were expected to sit. When the gallery could not accommodate the large numbers showing up for service, the rector, Rev. John Breynton, advised Black Anglicans to "meet in private homes." It may be safe to assume that the motivation for Blacks

---

135 Stephen Eric Davidson, *Black Loyalists in New Brunswick: The Lives of Eight African Americans in Colonial New Brunswick 1783-1834*, (Halifax, NS, Formac Publishing Co., Ltd., 2020), 80.

136 Davidson, op.cit., 80-81. Davidson points out that the Black Loyalists in New Brunswick fared better economically. A handful managed to achieve a middle-class status despite being barred by Saint John's charter of incorporation from living or working within the town.

joining the Anglican Church was more a matter of political and social advancement rather than religious conviction.

Back in Great Britain, Church of England officials did take an interest in the welfare of the newly freed Black Loyalists and enquired about their progress. The Archbishop of Canterbury wrote to enquire of Bishop Charles Inglis, Nova Scotia's first Anglican Bishop, to ascertain how the free settlers were progressing. In his reply, Inglis expressed optimism and expected the Black Loyalists to "prove to be equal to whites of the same rank."[137] Though Anglicans would prove to be the most generous of the churches in caring for the Black Loyalists through such societies as the Associates of the late Dr. Bray and the SPG, this benevolence did not translate into religious or social equality.

In addition to food and clothing (without which many would have died), the Anglican Church provided funding for several Black schools and educational materials throughout Nova Scotia. Education for the Black Loyalists had always been a priority for the Anglican Church through its missionary agency the SPG. It opened its first school in 1785, two years after the founding of Birchtown. Its first teacher was Colonel Stephen Blucke, who was biracial. Although the school was funded and staffed

---

137 James W. St. G. Walker, op. cit., 76.

by Anglicans, its thirty-six students held their classes in Birchtown's Methodist Meeting House.

Those teachers who deviated from the Anglican catechism were forced to conform or were fired. (Such had been the case with Black Loyalist school teacher, Catherine Abernathy, in Preston).[138] Black Loyalist teachers were nearly all Anglicans. Along with Abernathy, other known Black Loyalist teachers included Thomas Brownspriggs, Isaiah Limerick, Joseph Leonard, and Stephen Blucke. Moreover, Black Anglicans were given priority and therefore stood a better chance of receiving relief than Blacks who were members of other denominations.

In addition to meeting in their homes, Black Anglicans began conducting their own services without White supervision. In Birchtown, Isaac Limerick officiated as Reader and Exhorter. In Brindley Town, Joseph Leonard, not only conducted services, but performed baptisms and served communion—much to the shock and dismay of Anglican Church officials. Thomas Brownspriggs was both a teacher and preacher in Little Tracadie.

---

138 Because a church had not yet been built in the Preston Township, Abernathy held church services in her home. As an Anglican, she was expected to instruct her students in the Anglican catechism. Instead, she was accused of "embracing strange religious tenets." This accusation resulted in her salary being withheld. We are not told what these 'strange religious tenets' were. Can we speculate that Abernathy may have been teaching the African Baptist oral tradition? After mending her ways, Abernathy's salary was reinstated.

Despite the early growth of independent Black Anglican congregations, this did not result in the permanent development of indigenous Black Anglican congregations. Commenting on this fact, historian James Walker wrote,

"The Blacks cannot be considered as having formed any integral part of the Anglican structure anywhere in the province."[139] Walker's observation is rather surprising given that many Black Loyalists joined the Anglican Church in such large numbers in the eighteenth-century.

The Nova Scotia of the eighteenth-century must be seen against the backdrop of the Great Awakening. The Church of England was not the only denomination competing for the allegiance of the Black Loyalists community. There were also Baptists and Methodists, Roman Catholics, Huntingdonians, and Henry Alline's New Light movement. In the end, it would be the Baptists and Methodists that would have the greatest impact on the religious, social, and political life of the Black Loyalists. It was an influence that would last into the twentieth-century.

By 1784, there were 200 African Methodists worshipping in the neighbouring communities of Shelburne and Birchtown.[140] Methodists differed markedly from Baptists, both in their approach to conversion and in their organizational structure.

---

139 James W. St. G. Walker, op. cit., 71.

140 Matthew Richey, *Memoir of Rev. William Black* (Halifax, NS, 1839), 128.

The Methodist Episcopal Church (founded by John and Charles Wesley in England during the Great Awakening) was hierarchical and Episcopal in its liturgy and polity. Unlike the African Baptist, African Methodists cannot trace their origins to any form of oral tradition.

As the parent body, the English Methodists established what was called the *General Conference* as the church's ruling authority. The African Baptists, on the other hand, had no comparable institutional structure; but instead taught that one needed to *seek* after God in the hope of "finding" Him: a radical departure from what was required by the Methodists.

The Methodists met in classes presided over by lay leaders and were called "societies." There was no telling of experiences or "what the Lord had done." Conversion for the African Methodists consisted of a combination of theological literacy and an emotional response, rather than what Baptists called a "conversion experience." African Methodist preacher, Boston King, who was put in charge of the Methodists Society at Preston by Rev. William Black,[141] recorded in his memoir that: "The work of religion began to revive among us, and many were convinced of the sinfulness of sin and turned from

---

141 The Rev.William Black was the first Methodist missionary sent to Nova Scotia in 1780, by John Wesley. He was the first to establish a church in Shelburne. In his Shelburne congregation there were many Black Loyalists. He was appointed presiding elder by Wesley and overseer of the Black Methodist churches.

the error of their ways."[142] King further describes the experience of being convicted of sin and the sinner's emotional response when he writes, "Some fell flat on the ground as if they were dead. Others cried out aloud for mercy."[143] King recognized his inadequacy in thinking that it was within "my power to turn them from their evil ways."

The African Baptists approach to conversion differed radically from that of the Methodists. For example, there was no sudden and uncontrollable outburst of emotion. Conversion for African Baptists (at least traditionally) have usually been a private matter; not something to be put on public display. Moreover, Methodists did not examine their candidates in the way Baptists had done.

John Wesley took note of the evangelistic enthusiasm of the Black Methodists at Birchtown, and in a letter to James Barry (a White Loyalist in Shelburne) wrote,

> *I doubt not that some of them can read. When, therefore, we send a preacher or two to Nova Scotia, we will send some books...and they never need books while I live. It will be well to give them all the assistance you can in every way.*[144]

Unlike the Baptists, Methodists were methodical and meticulous in their missionary endeavours.

---

142 *Memoir of Boston King* (Methodist Magazine, 1798), 158.

143 Ibid., 213.

144 James W. St. G. Walker, op. cit., 73.

They maintained good records and statistics, hence the name *Methodism*. Another distinction between African Baptists and African Methodists was the Methodist Church's policy of racial segregation. The practice of segregation during worship in White Methodist churches experienced by Black Methodists was not unlike that encountered by Black Anglicans. While on one of his many preaching tours, African Methodist preacher, John Ball, was forced to hold a separate service later in the day after the Methodist preacher, Rev. William Black, held a rally. Though White Methodists could attend Ball's rallies, he was not permitted to address their gatherings.[145] African Methodists were allowed to use White Methodist churches, but only at a separate hour. James Walker describes the African Methodists in Halifax as regular participants in the Methodist services, but being "confined to a segregated galley."[146] When Wesley visited Nova Scotia, Black Methodists were not invited to attend the regular worship service.[147]

Such religious hypocrisy notwithstanding, African Methodists did not abandon the Methodist Church. The practice of racial segregation, coupled with indifference, meant that Black Methodists were often without regular White supervision, which left them free to develop their own forms of worship,

---

145 Ibid., 74.

146 Ibid.

147 Black Loyalist.com (Black Loyalists: Our History, Our People, 2021), 1

doctrines, and liturgy.[148] By 1790, Nova Scotia had four African Methodist churches in the communities of Liverpool, Amherst, Yarmouth, and Halifax. The only remaining African Methodist Church, called the Highland African Methodist Episcopal Church, is located in Amherst, and whose continued existence is uncertain.

The African Baptists of Nova Scotia differed from African Methodists in several ways. The Baptists were not governed by a hierarchy, (i.e., they did not have bishops or overseers). They were self-governing and democratic, with each church exercising its own autonomy. African Baptists were accountable only to its membership rather than a denominational hierarchy. Every member had a voice and could participate freely in the affairs of its church. "David George and his Baptist church," writes Walker, "offered freedom on a scale beyond the reach of the other denominations working among the Black Loyalists."[149] It was the desire for freedom and the opportunity to manage their own churches that brought the African Baptists into existence.

The first ABC established in Shelburne began in the home of David George with six members, two of whom were George and his wife, Phyllis. Despite the

---

148 The author recalls several years ago while in Toronto visiting the African Methodist Church and felt that I was worshiping in an African Baptist church; there were many similarities. This may be attributed to the fact that many of the members were former Baptists.

149 James W. St. G. Walker, op. cit., 76.

initial numerical majority of the African Methodists, it would be the African Baptists that would ultimately come to dominate the social, religious and political life of Nova Scotia's Black community.

Although George's Shelburne fellowship began with only six members, the determining factor was quality rather than quantity. It is "where two or three are gathered together" that God is often in the midst. George's church is a good illustration of the parable of the mustard seed, "…which indeed is the least of all seed; but when it is grown it is greater than the herbs…."[150]

Secondly, George's preaching was more spontaneous, fiery, and less formal and methodical than that of his Anglican and Methodist counterparts. Like New Light evangelist, Henry Alline, who preached throughout Nova Scotia before the founding of George's Shelburne church, often drew the ire of the White religious establishment for his unrelenting attacks on their "worn-out religious forms." Alline had little patience with what he called the "externals of religion" and decried the "damage done by unconverted ministers, and legal professors."[151] Alline arrived in the province in 1776 and, by the time of his premature death in 1784, had founded several New Light chapels and had garnered a large following of Black congregants.

---

150 Matt. 13:32.

151 Ibid., 65

Thirdly, African Baptists differed from Methodists in that they did not practice racial segregation. From the very beginning, George's Baptist church included White members. The first two Whites who joined George's church were a William and Deborah Holmes from Jones Harbour. The practice of integrated worship would continue under the leadership of George's White successor, the Rev. John Burton, who arrived in Nova Scotia following the Loyalists migration to Sierra Leone, in 1792. Burton would reorganize George's Shelburne church and established the first Baptist church in Halifax in 1795, which included several Black families.[152]

The fact that the Holmes had joined George's church in Shelburne did not sit well with members of Shelburne's White community. On the day of the baptism Mrs. Holmes' sister organized a mob and tried to prevent Mrs. Holmes from being immersed. "Mrs. Holmes' sister," George records, "especially laid hold of her hair to keep her from going down into the water; but the justices commanded peace, and said that she should be baptized as she herself desired it."[153] Opposition against George would continue, forcing him to relocate to Birchtown for a time.

---

152 I. E. Bill, *Fifty Years With The Baptist Ministers and Churches of the Maritime Provinces of Canada* (Barnes and Company, Saint John, NB, 1880), 176.

153 John Rippon, op. cit., 479.

George records that the Holmes were "converted by reading scripture."[154] For George, when it came to the conversion experience, his emphasis was on subjective feelings, and he gave only minor consideration to externals such as the Bible. This did not diminish the centrality of the scriptures, however. As was shown earlier in his memoir, George stated that following his conversion "what I have in my heart, I can see again in Scripture."[155] What this statement seems to suggest is that only after George's conversion was he able to see in the Bible what he now had in his heart.

Perhaps the most important difference between African Baptists and African Methodists is the African Baptist oral tradition and its approach to conversion. While the African Methodists emphasized a more institutional, methodical approach to conversion, the African Baptists took an oral, less structured approach. As discussed earlier, there were three types of Black Baptist churches that emerged

---

154 In pointing out that the Holmes were converted by reading scripture, represents an important distinction from the practice of *seeking*. The role of the Bible in the African Baptist conversion experience is of secondary importance. It is believed that one can know the Bible from Genesis to Revelations and still not experience salvation: that 'knowing' the Bible does not save you. Knowing Christ is what saves you! There is an almost fetish devotion to the Bible among many contemporary evangelicals and lay Christians without any thought for the insights of Higher Biblical criticism and hermeneutics.

155 John Rippon, op. cit., 476.

from the Great Awakening: Plantation, Balcony, and Invisible Baptists. George's Shelburne church could be described as invisible Baptists.[156]

Despite the differences between African Baptists and African Methodists, both continued to operate within the framework of Protestant orthodoxy, and therefore in many respects did not differ from their White counterparts. The theology of the Black church, writes Paris, "is akin to orthodox Christian conservatism buttressed by a literalistic view of the Bible."[157] Notwithstanding the fact that many Black churches owned and operated their own publishing houses, "the potential to impact the Black church has not been realized because Blacks failed to attend critically to the nature of the thought that guided their activities."[158] "Black preachers", therefore "have had little influence on the content of the published study materials which appears divorced from the social reality of daily life."[159] Paris attributes this lack of influence to the "social gap" that resulted from the separation between the oral and written traditions in the Black community. What Paris means by oral (i.e., the artistry of preaching, music and song) in the Black Christian tradition is not what is meant by *oral*

---

156 In contrast to the more visible, institutional, organized churches, invisible Baptists are both a fellowship of believers and a fellowship of the *Spirit*, hence the hiddenness of God.

157 Peter J. Paris, *The Social Teachings of the Black Churches*, (Fortress Press, Philadelphia, 1985), 78.

158 Ibid.

159 Ibid.

in the conversion experience in the Black Baptist oral tradition.

Having learned that several hundred Black Loyalists had settled in Shelburne, David George went there in June, 1783, temporarily leaving his family in Preston. He records, "there were no houses then built, they were just clearing and preparing to erect a town."[160] George soon began preaching but not without opposition. In his memoir, George recalled, "Numbers of my people were here, but I found the White people were against me. White people, the justices, and all were in an uproar, and said that I might go out into the woods, for I should not stay there."[161] Pearleen Oliver points out that there were two factors contributing to opposition to George: "white people joining his church and his theology that ran counter to the dominant theology of the day."[162] This was only the beginning of the opposition that George would face from both Whites and Blacks. Given that Nova Scotia was a slave society at this time, George's race would no doubt have been a factor in the negative reaction to his preaching.

Before erecting a meeting-place, George moved to a clearing in the woods where he preached every night. Both Whites and Blacks came from far and

---

160 John Rippon, op. cit., 478

161 Ibid, 478.

162 Pearleen Oliver, *A Brief History of the Colored Baptists of Nova Scotia 1783-1953.* In Commemoration of the Centenary of the African United Baptist Association of Nova Scotia, 20.

near to hear him. George remembered: "...and a great number of White and Black people came, and I was overjoyed with having an opportunity once more of preaching the word of God, that after I had given out the hymn, I could not speak for tears."[163]

George preached every night, and on Sunday held his first Lord's Day service in what he describes as a picturesque location in "a valley between two hills, close by the river."[164] The numbers gathering to hear George were steadily increasing, but he was still without land, a house, or meeting place. He was soon offered land by a gentleman he had known in Savannah. Although the benefactor was not identified in George's memoir, he was told he could "have his lot to live upon as long as I would, and build a house if I pleased."[165] Without encouragement or financial support from a parent body, but with help from "worldly Blacks," George soon went to work cutting down trees, removing the bark, and erecting what he described as "a smart hut." This structure served both as George's home and church. People came every night for a month as if "they were coming for their supper."

One month after David George arrived in Shelburne, Governor John Parr visited the Loyalist settlement accompanied by George's family. The colonial governor provided George with six months

---

163 Ibid.

164 John Rippon, op. cit., 478.

165 Ibid.

worth of desperately needed provisions, and a quarter of an acre of land, providing him with a degree of security. In describing his lot, George stated, "It was a spot where there was plenty of water, and which I had before secretly wished for, as I knew it would be convenient for baptizing at any time."[166]

An assessment roll from this period listed George's occupation as minister. However, there is no record that George was ever compensated for his pastoral duties. Rather, he was driven by a passionate desire to proclaim the gospel, and he trusted that God would provide. By this time, Blacks living in Shelburne were divided into companies and employed in the construction of roads and government buildings. It is quite possible to surmise that when George was not engaged in ministerial duties or tending his farm, he did similar work.

George began his church in Shelburne with six members: himself, his wife Phyllis, brothers Sampson and John, and sisters Ossee and Dinah. Several months later he baptized nine more, and the congregation continued to increase. George later recalled "that we had then a day of hearing what the Lord had done; and I and my wife heard their experiences."[167] By the summer of 1784 the membership had grown to fifty members.

Shortly after the founding of George's church, a William and Ann Taylor (both White) emigrated to

---

166 John Rippon, op. cit., 478.

167 Ibid.

Shelburne from England. The Taylors were Baptists and members of John Rippon's church in London. They had heard of George and went to visit him. A true godsend, the Taylors provided George with much needed provisions. George recalls Mrs. Taylor's visit: "she came to my house when I was so poor that I had no money to buy any potatoes for seed, and was so good as to give my children somewhat, and me enough money to buy a bushel of potatoes."[168] George does not mention the Taylors by name as being members of his church. Baptist historian, David Benedict, wrote in 1813 that the Taylors joined George's church and that William Taylor probably served as a deacon.[169] Whether William Taylor served as a deacon in George's church is disputed by some historians.[170] Based on T. W. Smith's research, the Taylors may not have actually joined George's church. Whether the Taylors were members or not, what is not in dispute is that they were certainly supporters of George's church.

As a Black Baptist preacher George's life was often in danger. On one particular occasion while preaching, a group of disbanded soldiers entered his church threatening him if he continued. Undeterred

---

168 Grant Gordon, op. cit., 56.

169 Ibid.

170 Methodist Historian, T. W. Smith, in an article entitled *The Loyalist at Shelburne*, published in the late 1800s, writes, "a small Baptist church (George's) was also put up at an early date, as was also one owned by Mr. Taylor, an English General Baptist." (Gordon, p. 56).

by such threats, George continued preaching. In his memoir, he recounted that several Black families had houses on his lot. He writes,

> *But forty or fifty disbanded soldiers came with tackle of ships and turned my dwelling house, and every one of their houses, quite over; and the meeting house they would have burned down had not the ring-leader of the mob himself prevent it."*[171] *The soldiers returned to the church beating George with sticks and driving him into a nearby swamp. "I returned in the evening", George recalls, "and took my wife and children over the river to Birchtown where some Black people were settled.*[172]

George was forced to leave Shelburne because of a race riot that had erupted in the summer of 1784, driving many Blacks into Birchtown. It was the first race riot in North America. George would face further opposition upon his arrival in Birchtown, not from angry White mobs, but from fellow Black Loyalists. Birchtown was home to several hundred Black Methodists and Anglicans. It was the Methodist blind preacher, Moses Wilkinson, and Anglican exhorter, Isaac Limerick, who opposed George.[173] Still he was undaunted by such opposition, and eventually found a receptive audience

---

171 John Rippon, op. cit., 480.

172 Ibid.

173 James W. St. G Walker, op. cit., 75.

in Birchtown, where he was invited into homes to speak. George records,

> *I preached at Birchtown from the fall till about the middle of December, (1784) and was frequently hearing experiences, and baptized about twenty there....A little before Christmas, as my own color persecuted me there, I set off with my family, to return to Shelburne.*[174]

Upon his return to Shelburne, George found his house destroyed and his meeting house being used as a tavern. The tavern-keeper boasted, "The old negro wanted to make a heaven of this place, but I'll make a hell of it."[175] Regaining his church—which also became his temporary home—George started holding services once more. People began attending again. George's suffering and hardships would be rewarded by a great revival in the summer of 1785.

Much of George's success was attributed to his preaching ability and personal piety. John Clarkson, agent for the Sierra Leone Company, observed while attending one of George's services, "I never remember to have heard the Psalms sung so charmingly in my life before."[176] A white congregant described how those in attendance were so "overcome that the people could not refrain from crying out hosannas...and George himself was forced to interrupt his sermon

---

174 John Rippon, op. cit., 480.

175 Ibid.

176 James W. St. G. Walker, op. cit., 75.

for the tears streaming down his face."[177] New Light itinerant preacher, Harris Harding, visited George's church and explained in a letter to his sister, dated August 20, 1791, what he experienced,

> *Yesterday morning I attended David's Meeting, where as soon as I came I found about twenty or thirty made white in the blood of the Lamb- singing hosannas to the Son of David. Several of them frequently was obliged to stop and rejoice, soon after David began prayer, but was so overcome with joy was likewise obliged to stop, and turned to me with many tears like brooks rolling down his cheeks desiring me to call upon that worthy name that was like ointment poured down upon the Assembly...My soul was upon a Mount Zion."*[178]

In contrasting George's church to that of the White church, Harding further states: "In contrast to the spiritual coldness and darkness of the whites, David's church appears at times like a woman clothed with the sun.[179] Speaking of George's character, Baptist preacher, William Chipman, recalls hearing George preach as a youth,

> *His modesty, humility, and very deep solemnity struck me with awe...and could but draw the*

---

177 Ibid.

178 Grant Gordon, op. cit., 70.

179 Ibid., 69.

conclusion that he was a man of very deep piety.
Oh what veneration I felt for him as a man
of God![180]

As George's reputation as a dynamic preacher began to spread, he started receiving invitations to preach in nearby settlements that were without pastoral leadership. As an itinerant preacher, his missionary tours took him to such towns as Ragged Island (now called Lockeport), Horton (now Wolfville), Liverpool, Jones Harbour, Halifax, Preston (where the oral tradition would have the most lasting impact) and as far away as New Brunswick.

In the summer of 1785, George travelled to Ragged Island to preach "among some white people, who desired to hear the word."[181] Nova Scotia historian, George Edward Levy, states that the first Baptist converts were the result of George's efforts,[182] and that he may have been the first preacher to visit the settlement. One such convert was Elizabeth, the wife of Jonathan Locke ll. She travelled back to Shelburne with George, gave her experience to the church, and was baptized "along with two black sisters." Mrs. Locke also had a sister who was converted, but whose family prevented her from being baptized. George does not give the name of Mrs.

---

180 Ibid., 68.

181 John Rippon, op. cit., 480.

182 George Edward Levy, *The Baptists of the Maritime Provinces*, (Barnes-Hopkins Ltd., Saint John, NB, 1947), 56.

Locke's sister, but states that "she was the only one in his church that was not baptized". "When his circumstances are considered", writes Levy, "there're few, if any, more heroic and romantic figures among the pioneers than David George."[183]

In New Brunswick, where several hundred Black Loyalists had settled, George required a special license from the governor to preach. The requirement to have a license to preach was not uncommon. A 1786 New Brunswick law called an *Act for the Preserving the Church of England*, stated that,

> *No one might officiate at a public religious exercise in the colony without having taken the oath of allegiance and that no one could lead a religious exercise...without a license from the governor.*[184]

Needing a license to perform one's pastoral duties is still a requirement today. The only such license that has survived from New Brunswick's early days of settlement, it states,

> *I do hereby certify, that David George, a free Negro man, has permission from his Excellency the Lieutenant Governor, to instruct the black people in the knowledge, and exhort them to the practice of the Christian religion.*[185]

Though George claims that he did not feel called to preach to White congregations, he never passed up the opportunity to do so. True to the principles of the

183 Ibid.
184 Ibid., 65.
185 Ibid., 66.

Christian faith, George made no such distinctions. His pioneering Baptist work in New Brunswick caused him to later return to the colony, where he had appointed Peter Richards (one of his elders) as the exhorter.

George would encounter similar restrictions at Liverpool. In January of 1790, a committee met to consider whether outsiders should be allowed to use the New Light Meeting House. It was decided that New Light preachers were welcomed, but "if Black David, a Preacher from Shelburne comes, he is to have liberty to speak in the House...but not in the stated times of worship, and only those who wish to listen to a Black man need attend."[186] Despite such blatant racism, George would develop the largest following of any contemporary Baptist preacher, Black or White. He was described as "one of the most enlightened of the Black preachers."[187]

Nevertheless because George's theology "ran counter to the dominant Christian theology of the day" he faced increasing opposition from both Whites and Blacks. On one occasion George attempted to baptize a Mrs. Holmes, who had joined his church, when an angry mob gathered and tried to prevent her from being baptized. Mrs. Holmes' sister "laid hold of hair to keep her from going down into the water".[188] Such chaos ensued that local authori-

---

186 James w. St. G. Walker, op. cit., 77.

187 Grant Gordon, op. cit., 147.

188 Grant Gordon, op. cit., 60.

ties were summoned to restore order and allow the baptism to continue. Opposition to George became so fierce that he was forced to leave Shelburne. In his 1975 honours thesis, Nova Scotia historian and author, Stephen Davidson, may have been echoing a similar point, when he wrote, "Maritime historians have not examined the reasons for...the beliefs and practices of Black churches compared with White churches."[189]

What were some of the distinguishing characteristics of George's theology, and how did it differ from the dominant Christian theology of the day? One of the consistent themes running throughout George's theology was "what the Lord had done". George took no credit in bringing the unsaved to a knowledge of salvation. Conversion is the will and work of God; it is not a human endeavor. "Therefore the pastor and evangelist should not use 'means' or methods that would place human pressure on people", states George.[190] George believed that salvation was the work of God, and was opposed to the use of 'means', or human influence, such as the "instruction of children and family religion", which could not bestow grace. All such practices could lead to Pharisaism. Rather, it was only through an "inward feeling" that one could know if he/she was saved.

Such means are used today in most ABC when preparing candidates for baptism. Candidates are

189 Stephen Eric Davidson, op. cit., 7.

190 Grant Gordon, op.cit., 144

paired with an instructor (or church counsellor) and given instructional booklets called *New Life Classes*. For several weeks, candidates are taught from these booklets and schooled in the fundamentals of the Christian faith in preparation for baptism. Such instructions—however methodical and meticulous—cannot result in a personal encounter with God.

Another theme found in George's theology—and which was an integral part of his ministry—was the "hearing of experiences." His memoir states, "that we appointed a time every other week to hear experiences."[191] This was a constant expression running throughout George's memoir. What he does not disclose is the content and nature of these conversion experiences. As later generations would show, there was an element of secrecy in the telling of one's conversion. Hence, it was only those having a similar experience who were allowed to hear the experience of another. The telling of one's experience was considered so sacred that it was seldom told even to fellow-believers. No two experiences are ever the same and the effect is so profound and life-changing that the experience is never forgotten. "Jesus I'll never forget what you've done for me! Jesus I'll never forget how you set me free!..." is how one spiritual went.

In taking a closer look at the finer points of David George's theology, Grant Gordon has provided us with a rather detailed theological exchange between

---

191 John Rippon, op. cit., 479.

George and Zachary Macaulay.[192] The discussion took place after George had migrated to Sierra Leone, where he lived during his senior years. Nevertheless, the beliefs George held at that time would have been the same as those he espoused during his ministry in Nova Scotia.

Though the discussion is told from Macaulay's perspective, and is found recorded in his journal, it does still reveal much of George's theological thought. Given the limited scope of this project, I will look only briefly at the debate between the two men. Macaulay felt George was too secure in his salvation and that his theology was "unscriptural" and his doctrines "abominable."[193] He pointed to certain sins within George's congregation, such as "drunkenness, neglect of family religion, instruction of children, and unchastity"[194] as the result of the lack of sound Biblical teaching. He accused George of antinomianism—the dependence on grace rather than adhering to a strict set of moral principles. Antinomianism can be best understood as anti-law; that is, depending of God's grace rather than reducing Christianity to a legalistic set of moral rules and regulations to which Christians were bound. Antinomianism is the belief that despite moral lapses into sin and ungodliness, one can still be certain of his/her salvation.

---

192 Zachary Macaulay was a young Scotsmen and the son of a Church of Scotland minister. He came to Sierra Leone in 1793, to serve on the council and to assist Governor William Dawes.
193 Grant Gordon, op. cit., 144.
194 Ibid.

Macaulay, however, took the opposite view. "The Antinomian scheme," he wrote, "is a most seducing one: no means to be used, no exertions to be made, no lusts to be crucified, no self-denial to be practiced."[195] Macaulay cited a sermon by George, in which he heard him say, "It is not for every little sin as being overtaken by drunkenness, or some temptation, that a Child of God is to lose his interest in Christ; once in Christ, always in Christ; whom God loves, He loves to the end."[196] George argued that salvation was God's work not that of the individual.

In quoting several passages from the Bible to make his point, Macaulay felt he had gained the upper hand. He then asked George what he thought was "the rule of faith and practice?" George responded: "It must be the written word"; but insisted on the "Spirit within." George believed that it was only through inward feeling that one knows if one is saved.[197] In describing the "indwelling" of the Holy Spirit as an inward feeling, George may have been foreshadowing the later thought of the gifted nineteenth-century

---

195 Ibid., 146

196 Ibid.

197 Grant Gordon, op. cit., 143. What both Macaulay and George didn't seem to know or appreciate (and what Paris has pointed out in his insightful book *The Spirituality of African Peoples*) that in African culture there is no rigid separation between the sacred and the secular as in Western culture: that all reality is a reflection of God. That the cosmos is pervaded by the sacred. This helps to explain how Christians in the Black community can be guilty of moral indiscretions and still be considered Christian.

Danish theologian, Soren Kierkegaard, who held that truth was "subjective" or what he called "inwardness."[198] Based on such reasoning, God can only be known subjectively but never objectively (i.e., through means).

The doctrinal differences between George and Macaulay may not have been only theological, but cultural. The fact that Macaulay was European and a man of privilege, and George born a second-generation slave, no doubt contributed to their sharp differences. Moreover, Macaulay was also an evangelical Christian and a member of the Established Church of Scotland. Part of his responsibility was the establishment of schools for religious education—he being one of the instructors. Such a position, therefore, made him "skeptical of some forms of sudden conversion." George, on the other hand, came out of a less literate, oral tradition that was less structured. Macaulay, on the other hand, was always "skeptical of some forms of sudden conversion."

Despite all that David George had to endure as a preacher of the gospel (beaten, forced to relocate, the loss of his house), the hidden hand of providence continued to sustain him. Historian, George Edward Levy, wrote of George: "None came here [Nova Scotia] with less in his favour, none left with more to his credit."[199] The seed of the African Baptist

---

198 Soren Kierkegaard, *Concluding Unscientific Postscript*, (Princeton University Press, New Jersey,1941), 68.

199 George Edward Levy, op. cit., 58.

Church was sown in the soil of suffering; its fruit, however, would not be realized until the nineteenth-century. Because George appointed elders in two of the churches he founded (Saint John and Preston) it is safe to assume that these churches practised the oral tradition.

David George's work and legacy would experience a hiatus until the arrival of the refugees resulting from the War of 1812—most of whom were staunch Baptists. It would be under the leadership of Reverend Richard Preston that the old time religion would be resurrected and have its greatest impact.

Chapter Four

Richard Preston and the African Baptist Refugees

The pastoral leadership vacuum left by the exodus of Black Loyalist preachers to Sierra Leone was filled by the Reverend John Burton. A White Methodist missionary, Burton arrived in Nova Scotia with his family from Durham, England, in 1792. He was a licensed dissenting[200] minister under the sponsorship of the *Countess of Huntingdon*, a wealthy benefactress and supporter of the Methodist cause. Burton was on his way to the United States and only planned to stay in Halifax for a short time. After his arrival in the city, he was invited to preach by Philip

---

200 Dissenting ministers were those who disagreed with the doctrines and practices of the established church. In Burton's case it would the Anglican Church.

Marchington,[201] a merchant who had built a meeting house for the Methodists in the city. (This was the same meeting house where, four months earlier, David George gave his farewell sermon before departing for Sierra Leone).

In the fall of 1793, Burton made a trip to the United States where he converted to the Regular Baptist doctrine: a doctrine based on the *Philadelphia Confession of Faith*[202], and was baptized by immersion. After completing further studies, he was re-ordained as a Baptist minister.

Burton returned to Nova Scotia in January, 1794, a changed man—much to the surprise and dismay of the Methodists—including Brother Marchington. Burton's decision to convert to the Baptist faith may have already taken place prior to travelling to the United States. If that was the case, his trip may have simply been to complete the process of accreditation and ordination within the Baptist denomination.

In 1795, Burton founded the first Baptist church in Halifax, located on the corner of Barrington and

---

201 Philip Marchington arrived in Halifax from New York as a Loyalist, in 1783. He was a wealthy merchant, member of the Legislative Assembly, and a devout Methodist.

202 The *Philadelphia Confession of Faith* was the first published doctrinal statement by Baptists in North America and was printed in 1742. It adhered to a strict Calvinist theology and was one of the most influential confessions among Baptists.

Buckingham Streets.[203] Known as Burton's Church, its membership consisted largely of Black Baptists and poor, lower-class Whites. In the year that the church was officially dedicated, it had thirty-three members. "Despised, or simply tolerated in the other churches of the colony," in Burton's church "the black man found a warm welcome…and had the opportunity to join its membership."[204] This "warm welcome" by Burton, notwithstanding, the Maritime Baptist Association admonished Burton "not to fraternize too freely with blacks, not to sleep in their homes, eat with them or allow unqualified elders to preach."[205] Such behaviour, it was felt, would result in harm being done to both Blacks and Whites, and would change the "natural order of society."

African Nova Scotian author and entrepreneur, Frank Boyd, cited an article in the *Christian Visitor* magazine, dated July 16, 1856, writing "one gets the impression that Burton was regarded by his white Baptist colleagues as a man of insufficient ability to minister to whites, but that he was of use ministering

---

203 The churches founded by David George in Nova Scotia did not necessarily consist of a visible, institutional structure, but instead were congregations of assembled believers (i.e., where there are two or three gathered together) called the invisible church. It would take the arrival of Burton to organize George's churches into a visible, organized structure.

204 Stephen Eric Davidson, op. cit., 30.

205 Bridglal Pachai, *Beneath The Clouds of the Promise Land: The Survival of Nova Scotia's Blacks, vol. 2*, (Lancelot Press Ltd., Hantsport, Nova Scotia), 54.

to blacks."[206] The Rev. I. E. Bill, writing at the time, paints a more positive picture of Burton's church, describing it as "respectable and well established." He wrote, "A respectable congregation has been collected, from which Mr. Burton receives a comfortable support."[207] However, Bill further states "He was not eloquent; as a denominational man he was not prominent; but in the depth of an all-pervading piety, and in the fullness of devotion to his life work, he had no superior, and but few equals."[208]

With the arrival of some 2000 refugees between 1813 and 1815 as a result of the War of 1812—most of whom were Baptists—membership in Burton's Baptist church swelled to almost 300. Most of the men were described as labourers, farmers, tradesmen, sawyers, shoemakers, and wheelwrights.[209]

After establishing his church in Halifax, Burton began his missionary and pastoral work among the Baptist congregations established by George, including Shelburne and Ragged Island (now Lockeport). The church at Shelburne had dissolved following the migration to Africa, and the members who did not leave were without a church or leader. Burton re-established the church at Shelburne, but over time

---

206 Peter E. McKerrow, *A Brief History of Blacks in Nova Scotia*, (Ed. by Frank Stanley Boyd, Jr., 1975, originally printed by Nova Scotia Printing Co., 1895), 111. The author has not been able to substantiate this article.

207 I. E. Bill, op. cit., 33.

208 Ibid, 177.

209 Bridglal Pachai, op. cit., 22.

it would become a predominantly White congregation. This pastoral field also included the church at Lockeport. The churches at Jones Harbour and Saint John, New Brunswick, were abandoned following the Black Loyalists' exodus to Sierra Leone. With the arrival of the refugees between the years 1813-1815, Burton's ministry would expand to include the Black refugee communities of Hammonds Plains, Preston, Beech Hill (now Beechville), Cherry Brook/Lake Loon, and Dartmouth.

Like all pioneering pastors of the nineteenth-century, John Burton was given the honorific title "Father" by his Black congregants. Burton had no equals when it came to the spiritual welfare and paternalistic concerns of the Black communities. His compassion and influence were such that civil authorities gave him the sole responsibility of attending to the affairs of the Baptist refugees. This responsibility extended to serving as a magistrate in deciding disputes between Blacks. One observer, who felt Rev. Burton was uniquely qualified, wrote,

> *Brother Burton was just the man to have the care and management of this class of people, the coloured. There is something peculiar in them, and there was something in the preacher which qualified him to deal with them. Brother B. was a king among them....He reigned with undisputed sway amongst them. He said come, and they came, go and they went, do this, and they did it; but if he was a king, he was a fatherly king; for in his*

government, he united the mildness and condescen-
sion of a father with the severity of the sovereign.
Father Burton used to exercise the office of
magistrate in connection with that of a pastor. He
cited delinquent persons before him...and without
any jury; he gave his judgement against the evil
doer. This was done not only with the members of
his church but with others, and all submitted to
his decision.[210]

Despite Burton's unparalleled influence in the development of the ABC, what is conspicuously absent is the oral tradition first established by George and the hearing of experiences. Burton's indifference to the church's tradition is revealed in an exchange between himself and a member at a conference held in Chester in 1834. The member (whose name is not given) wanted to share with Burton how the grace of God was working in his life. When the member proceeded to tell Burton about a dream he had had, Burton stopped him and said, "I will come and see you one of these days, when I will hear all about your dream. But I wish you now to tell us how it was with you when you were awake."[211] It appears that Burton may have been aware of the church's oral tradition, but felt that it was not the time or place to hear one's experience.

---

210 Peter E. McKerrow, op. cit., 10.

211 J. M. Cramp, *The Baptist of Nova Scotia, 1760-1860*, (scrapbook of edited columns, Acadia University, Special Collections), 252.

Despite this instance of not wanting to hear the member's experience, Burton would continue much of George's legacy of personal evangelism, ordination of elders and pastors, and the integration of the races--a policy first established by David George. It is difficult, however, to determine to what extent the other churches served by Burton (Preston, Hammonds Plains, Dartmouth, Cherry Brook, Beech Hill, Campbell Road) were integrated. With the arrival of Richard Preston these churches would become predominantly Black congregations.

Burton's Baptist polity and practice was typical of the times, and not unlike other White Regular Baptist churches in the colony. He "kept unmarred the strict doctrine and practice of a Baptist church." Their unity was "maintained by their adherence to a revised form of the *Philadelphia Confession of Faith*...and by their lower class status."[212] The emphasis was on an "external order" rather than on an inward experience.

Major doctrinal disputes among White Baptists often had to do with the sacraments and the status of unbaptized members. The issue of the unbaptized receiving communion was finally resolved in 1809 when it became church policy that only those baptized were to become members. It was not until this policy was accepted as the given practice of the Association that Burton's church joined the Regular Baptist Association. "All of the members and

---

212 Philip G. A. Allwood, *First Baptist Church, Halifax, Its Origin and Early Years*, (Master of Divinity Thesis, Acadia University, 1978), 76.

ministers," wrote Davidson, "had to have been baptized into the church membership by immersion."[213] It was not until 1811, the year before Burton became moderator of the Maritime Baptist Association, that his Halifax church united with the Association.

Burton's church stood alone in refusing to join the Association until the "non-Regular Baptists were expelled," that is to say, those churches that admitted members who were not baptized by immersion. Between 1818 and 1819 more than two hundred were baptized in Burton's church. In1832 twenty more entered the waters of baptism.[214] Yet ironically Burton's "rigid standards and strict adherence to Baptist principles" did not prevent the eventual demise of his church; in fact, it may have been the cause of it—due to the failure of Burton to build on the foundation first laid by George—that is to say, on the church's oral tradition.

New Light preacher, Henry Alline, described the sacraments of baptism and communion as "externals," and did not consider them overly important. "He baptized but little himself," wrote Bill, "and never

---

213 Stephen Eric Davidson, op. cit., 36

214 Much is made today of the sacrament of water baptism. Aside from being a public acknowledgment and confession of one's faith in Jesus Christ as Lord and Saviour, and producing a good conscience toward God, baptism itself has no saving power. Rather, it is the "second baptism" of the Holy Spirit (Matt. 3:11) that has saving power, but never gets the attention it warrants. Moreover, baptism symbolizes the burial and resurrection of Christ and the rising again to a new life in Christ.

condescended to go into the water; but was willing his followers should practice whatever mode they chose...."[215] Like his successor, David George, Alline focused on what took place internally, not externally. The importance of baptism by immersion was not an issue for Alline or George. Rather, it was whether a person was truly *saved*. For Alline, "theology was always personal...and subject to the test of feeling and experience."[216] It is the subjectivity of feeling that aptly describes the African Baptist conversion experience. Baptism by immersion, therefore, could be seen as secondary and not an issue to be debated.

Unlike his predecessor, Richard Preston left no record of his conversion experience. We do know that he was converted on a Virginia plantation in 1815, where he preached for a brief time. He was bi-racial, of manly bearing, and stood six feet, one inch tall. Preston purchased his freedom; and in 1816, arrived in Nova Scotia in search of his mother. He would eventually find her living in the refugee community of Preston. Consequently, he adopted the name Preston as his surname. The fact that Preston came from the same colony of Virginia as George, and eventually settled in Preston, it is safe to assume that he had undergone a similar conversion experience. Preston, therefore, would play a significant role in helping to

---

215 I.E. Bill, op. cit., 13--14.

216 Maurice Armstrong, *The Great Awakening in Nova Scotia*, (The American Society of Church History, Hartford, Connecticut, 1948), 93.

"maintain the historical identity and continuity" of the oral tradition in the Preston community.

By the time of the arrival of the African Baptist refugees, the church's oral tradition had become nonexistent in Nova Scotia. The Black Loyalists who did not journey to Sierra Leone either joined other denominations or simply discontinued the practices of the oral tradition. Preston's arrival may have been providential in that it sparked a revival among African Baptists.

Like most African Baptists arriving in Nova Scotia during this time, Preston joined Burton's church. It was not long before Burton recognized Preston's potential for ministry and leadership. He soon took the young Virginian under his wing and began to groom him. Though limited in education, "he was of ready wit, humorous, and a good extemporaneous speaker."[217] After several years of pastoral and apprenticeship training under Burton, Preston was licensed in 1823, and given the pastoral responsibilities of the Black Baptist churches once served by Burton.

The split that would ultimately develop between Burton and Preston resulted in the founding of the Cornwallis Street Baptist Church. Burton alleged that the differences between himself and Preston

---

217 Peter E. McKerrow, op. cit., 16.

were theological and based on a "false doctrine."[218] Could it be that Burton's charge of a "false doctrine" was in fact the oral tradition? Davidson, on the other hand, contends that the issue was one of "race" rather than theology.[219] The facts, however, do not seem to support such a claim given that Burton was an integrationist, and Preston "encouraged interracial cooperation," resulting in the appointment of a White successor in the person of Rev. James Thomas.[220]

As was already mentioned, not all ABCs practised its founder's religious tradition. Moreover, because this tradition was oral, it did not get included in the official church records. Instead what one sees

---

218 Both Davidson (Acadia Univ. honours thesis,1975, p 47) and Boyd (Dictionary of Canadian Biography, 2), state that the rupture between Preston and Burton was the result of racial tensions between Black and White members who had recently left St Paul's Anglican Church. There was an attempt by White members to have Black congregants removed.

219 Stephen Eric Davidson, op. cit.,70

220 James Thomas was from Wales, United Kingdom. He immigrated with his parents (his mother was Jewish) to Nova Scotia at the age of twelve (The actual year is unknown). The family were devoted Baptists and settled in the Preston Township, where they became members of the African Baptist Church. Thomas married a Black women by the name of Hannah Saunders, giving birth to six children. He became good friends with Richard Preston and began traveling with him throughout the province. Thomas was ordained by Preston in 1857. Thomas is also the great-great-grand father of the author.

are passing references.[221] This can also be seen in Burton's reaction to a member who wanted to share his experience during an 1834 conference in Chester and the encounter between African Baptist, William Redman, in Preston, and Anglican missionary, Rev. William Nisbett, which will be seen momentarily.

Only those who had undergone a similar experience could hear the testimony of the candidate. This element of secrecy can also be seen in the teachings of Jesus when telling his disciples that "...it has been given to you to know the mysteries [hidden truth] of the kingdom of heaven, but to them it has not been given."[222] Jesus also instructed His disciples to pray to God in secret. Jesus' ministry was both public and private. What he said publicly, he would then explain to his disciples privately.[223] There was an element of secrecy among African Baptists in not sharing their experience with non-members.

We noted in a previous chapter that three types of ABCs emerged from the Great Awakening of

---

221 In the 1903 annual minutes of the African Baptist Association, St. Thomas and Cherry Brook churches reported receiving new members by experience. It does not, however, explain the nature of these "experiences" (p19). In 1917, Licentiate W. B. Thomas stated at the annual AUBA session that he "found the Lord in the East Preston Baptist Church." However, Thomas does not elaborate on what 'finding the Lord' entailed. The point is that Thomas did not say 'I accepted the Lord', which is commonly (even today) what is usually stated.

222 Matt. 13:11.

223 Matt. 24:3, Mk. 9:28, 13:3, Lk. 9:10

the eighteenth-century. It was the Invisible Baptist Church represented by George, however, that would first be established in Nova Scotia.[224] In describing Preston's evangelistic work in the community of Preston (where he resided), author and former clerk of the AUBA, Peter E. McKerrow, wrote: "His religious views were entirely in keeping with their own."[225] *Their own* being that of the oral tradition. Why Preston's evangelistic work in other African Baptist communities was not the same as that in Preston is hard to explain.

When the African Baptists refugees arrived in Nova Scotia from the United States, and were questioned about their religion and how they acquired it, their response was, "It was in the forest, behind the stone walls, in the cotton fields, and rice swamps."[226] As African Baptists, whose faith was invisible, it represented a hidden, spiritual presence (hence the name *invisible*). It is a "spiritual presence" that is not visible in the official institutional ABC.[227] Moreover, in addition to being hidden, such faith is seldom found within the majority. Because God, therefore,

---

224 With the exception of the Preston-area churches (East and North Preston, Cherry Brook/Lake Loon, and Africville) none of the African Baptist churches served by Richard Preston appear to have practised an oral tradition.

225 Peter E. McKerrow, op. cit., 58.

226 Ibid, 11.

227 Baptist churches both in England and Nova Scotia were of two major types: General Baptist and Particular Baptist. The Particular Baptist (who were Calvinists) represented the Invisible Church.

is hidden, mysterious, and invisible, He must be seen through the eyes of faith. Hence, "for we walk by faith not by sight."[228] To walk by faith rather than by sight is to live a life of doubt and uncertainty. It is to take risk with the potential to fail.

In making the distinction between the visible and invisible church, in 1869 the Rev. James Thomas, then moderator of the African Baptist Association, presented the *Statement of Faith and Practice Concerning a Visible Church of Christ and its Discipline*. It stated in part

> *A particular visible Church of Christ, is a number of his saints, by mutual acquaintance and communion voluntarily and understandingly covenanting and embodying together, for upholding and promoting the worshiping and service of God, to show forth his declarative glory, and for their own edification.*[229]

What this demonstrates is the merging of the visible and invisible African Baptist Church. Moreover, in terms of *Baptist Polity and Practice* and Protestant orthodoxy, African Baptists in general did not differ radically from their White Baptists counterparts. In 1832, (the year it was founded by Preston) the Cornwallis Street Baptist Church adopted the "Articles of Faith and Practice" of the Nova Scotia

---

228 2 Cor. 5:7.

229 Minutes of the Sixteenth Session of the annual African Baptist Association, 1869.

Baptist Association, and applied for membership.[230] In 1884 the AUBA joined the Maritime Baptist Convention and sent delegates to its annual conferences. In 1840 there were seven ABCs in Nova Scotia, consisting of 273 members. In 1854 (at its founding) the AUBA had twelve churches, and a membership of 308. By 1897 there were twenty-two churches, with a membership 2,440; and by 1953 the AUBA could claim ten thousand adherents.[231] And by the first decade of the twentieth-century, ninety percent of Nova Scotia's Black population were African Baptists; by 1961, more than ten percent of the province's Baptists were African Baptists.[232] Current data on the number of African Baptists in the province within its eighteen churches are not available.

Efforts by Richard Preston in calling both Refugees and the Black Loyalists—those who had not joined the exodus to Sierra Leone—back to their southern religious origins was essential to their identity as a people. However, proselytizing by the Anglican Church often hampered these efforts. Many Black Loyalists who remained in Nova Scotia, and who were adherents of the Baptist faith, eventually

---

230 Philip G. A. Griffin-Allwood, "*Reason to Be: A Response to System Racism*" (A paper presented at a joint workshop of the African United Baptist Association and the Convention of Atlantic Baptist Churches, 2007), 5.
231 Robin W. Winks, *The Blacks in Canada*: A *History*, 2nd ed, (McGill-Queen's University Press, Montreal, Que., 1971), 346.
232 Ibid.,

abandoned their Baptist roots and began attending White churches, the Anglican Church in particular.

In 1825 the Anglican Church appointed a catechist at Preston in the person of the Rev. William Nisbett, in an attempt to instruct the Baptist Refugees in tenets of the Christian faith. Nisbett soon discovered in Preston what Anglican missionary Archibald Gray had found among the refugees at Hammonds Plain: they were staunch Baptists. Bishop John Inglis described the Preston refugees as a "peculiar people"; but then added, "The majority of the Blacks, however ignorant, are rigid Baptists and will not come to Church nor receive favours through the Church."[233]

Neither the War of 1812 Refugees nor the Black Loyalists responded to the Anglican missionary efforts in large numbers. The religious tradition of the African Baptist refugees was an exclusive faith that contributed to their separation from both the larger White society—upon whose charity they were dependent— and from the Black Loyalist community, many of whom had become Anglican.

As an Anglican who came from a European culture and background, Nisbett was indifferent (if not diametrically opposed) to the African Baptists' way of experiencing God. One such incident was when William Redman, a Preston resident, shared with Nisbett a somewhat graphic experience on two

---

233 James W. St. G. Walker, op. cit., 90.

separate occasions of "seeing a person on a cross whom he had stabbed with a knife, drawing blood and water."[234] For African Baptists the role of the blood of Christ stands at the very centre of its oral tradition. Nisbett condemned such notions and described the refugees as "universally superstitious, mad, ridiculous, and given to monstrous absurdities...in the place of religion."[235]

Nisbett's attitude and response to the religious practices of African Baptists were typical of the times and of organized religion generally. Yet it was these types of experiences as expressed by Redman that ultimately determined whether one was *saved*. Frustrated and impatient with his work in Preston, Nisbett left for Bermuda in1829 to work with the *Society for the Conversion of the Negroes.*

Richard Preston's break with John Burton and the founding of the *Cornwallis Street African Baptist Church* in 1832, marked a turning point in the relationship between White and Black Baptists in the colony. African Baptist churches are forever indebted to the pioneering and dedicated work of the Rev. John Burton who stepped into the breach left by George's departure. The history of Burton's unselfish devotion to the African Baptist community, and his eventual demise as one of its outstanding leaders remains to be written.

---

234 Robin W. Winks, op. cit., 138.

235 Ibid.

Despite the succession of pastors that served on the Preston field[236] after the death of Preston, the oral religious practices continued up until the pastorate of Rev. Donald D. Skeir, which began in 1953.[237] Unlike David George, we do not have any memoirs or written conversion experiences of pastors who served the Preston churches—most of whom were not from Preston—or how they may have viewed the church's traditional beliefs and practices.[238]

---

236 The Preston field in the nineteenth-century consisted of three churches: First Preston Church (which today is the East Preston Baptist Church, Second Preston Church, located today in North Preston, and whose named was later changed to St. Thomas in 1879; and Third Preston Church, called Fulton Church, located then on Frog Lake Road. The communities of Lake Loon and Cherry Brook did not have an actual church building until 1902, even though Richard Preston founded a church there in 1844. Before constructing their own church, the community worshipped at East and North Preston, where many were baptized and held membership. When the church did not travel to East and North Preston, they worshipped in their homes. You might say the church in Lake Loon and Cherry Brook represented the Invisible Church. The pastors who would have served in Preston when it constituted one field after Richard Preston's death would have included the Reverends James Thomas, his son, John Thomas, Jacob Allan, Benson Smithers, Charles Roan, George Carvery, George Neale, Edward Dixon, John Smith, Wellington States, William White, Andrew Morgan, and Arthur Wyse. Rev. Donald D. Skeir would be the last pastor to serve the Preston churches as one field (1953--1995.)

237 Cherry Brook United Baptist Church 90th anniversary booklet, published in 1992.

238 Our sources tell us that the only pastors born in Preston were: Rev. Arthur Wyse, Rev. Benson Smithers, and Rev. George Carvery.

One pastor of particular interest from Preston was Rev. Wyse. Rev. Wyse was born in the community of Lake Loon, in 1867, the same year Canada officially became a country. He was converted in 1893. Rev. Wyse is of significance because he represented the last of the Preston-area pastors born in the nineteenth-century, and was one of the fourteen founding members of the Cherry Brook Baptist Church, which was officially dedicated in 1902. With only four days of formal schooling, Rev. Wyse's powerful preaching and inspiration came directly from the Holy Spirit. He was pastor of the Preston field churches from 1910 to 1953—the longest of any serving pastor.

Because we have the testimony of those who knew Rev. Wyse, it is safe to assume that he followed the traditional path of conversion.[239] He may have been the last pastor who practised and preached the oral tradition in the Preston-area churches. Rev. Wyse died at the ripe old age of eighty-six, in 1953. He was succeeded by Rev. D.D. Skeir in 1953.

Rev. Skeir was born in Halifax and was a graduate of Acadia University, where he majored in history. He was employed in the public school system for

---

239 Those interviewed for this project (some of whom were converted under Rev. Wyse's preaching) spoke fondly of him as a powerful and dynamic preacher. One elder shared that Rev. Wyse would pace the floor all night agonizing over his call to preach and his sense of unworthiness. Rev. Wyse's pastorate in Cherry Brook only lasted until 1918. He would return in 1949, four years before his death.

twenty-seven years. Rev. Skeir was a Methodist before converting to the Baptist faith and served in many capacities within the AUBA, including as moderator and clerk.

Because the deacons played such a dominant role as overseers of the conversion process, the church's tradition was never publicly challenged. This practice would continue under Rev. Skeir's pastorate for the next twenty years. In 1976, Rev. Skeir would perform the largest baptism in the history of the Preston field when 110 candidates would go down into the waters of baptism. Rev. Skeir's passing in 1995 represented the end of an era in that he was the last pastor to serve the Preston churches as one field.

Things began to change as time passed and the older deacons were deceased. By the 1980s, less people were setting out *to pray*. Under Rev. Skeir's ministry, more and more individuals were now being baptized "on the profession of their faith" rather than through a conversion experience. Though the spirituals continued to be sung and the words of certain prayers that reflect the old-time religion could still be heard, the faith that produced such spirituals and prayers were no longer practised.

Moving away from the traditional approach to conversion to the modern approach can often result in polarization and heated exchanges between the "traditionalists" and those who did not come the traditional way.

Chapter Five

The Conversion Experience
(seeking, finding, and knowing)

The previous chapters have attempted to show that the African Baptist oral tradition is thoroughly Christian, and that its genesis can be traced back to the Old Testament. This last chapter will explain in more detail the conversion process in the African Baptist oral tradition. It should also be pointed out that in explaining the conversion experience, we are relying on what the elders have shared. More importantly, it will show the centrality of the blood of Christ in that experience.

If there is one passage of scripture that sums up the importance of salvation in the African Baptist oral tradition, it is Mark 8:36: "For what will it profit a man if he gains the whole world and loses his own soul?" Jesus goes on to say in this text: "Is anything worth more than your soul?" What these passages suggest is that there is nothing more important in life than getting saved from one's sinful state. Whether it is material success, wealth, social class, or economic status, none of these are a greater priority than "getting your soul converted." While adhering to the historic doctrines of the Christian faith, and being an integral part of the institutional structures of the ABC, the Preston-area churches, which include the community of Cherry Brook, took a more radical approach to salvation than that practised by other Black Baptist churches. While the latter practised a "Biblical Christianity," the Preston churches practised an "experiential Christianity".

Unlike other ABCs—and Baptist churches generally—it was not enough simply to believe. Nor merely to invite Jesus Christ into one's life as Lord and Saviour. In the African Baptist oral tradition, such an approach to salvation fell far short of what the church required. Yet, it has been the more popular, conventional approach to salvation that is now practised by Baptist churches generally both African and White.

Instead, the oral approach consists of *seeking, finding,* and *knowing* the Lord. It meant knowing God for oneself in an intimate and personal way.[240] It required going into one's secret closet and spending time in solitude and continued prayer. The oral

240 At a time when the existence of God is being constantly challenged (especially by the New Atheists), and the influence of organized religion in Canada is waning, belief in a personal God seems all the more absurd.

tradition includes the fundamental belief that a failure to seek the Lord, to find Him, or know Him, was the worst of all spiritual states, the implication being that one was a "hell-deserving sinner" in need of repentance. The earlier one found the Lord, the better.[241] If one did nothing else in life, one was expected and admonished to *pray*.

Not everyone, however, complied with the church's founding tradition and its strict criteria for salvation. There were those who felt such rules were unnecessary, and that they were man-made. Those failing to submit to the church's teachings were denied membership. The denial of church membership often had a generational effect that resulted in people joining other churches that did not have such exclusive policies—or in some cases never joining any church. Such restrictions, the oral tradition maintained, were not to prevent a person from joining the church. Rather, they were to ensure that the individual's conversion was genuine (i.e., that it was of God and not of the individual). It was imperative to have a truly genuine conversion, to get it right the first time. It was important to ascertain that the individual had actually experienced God's grace and forgiveness. This required more than a personal testimony as is the case today. According to the tenets of the oral

---

241 People were often encouraged to seek the Lord while they were in their youth: "To remember your Creator in the days of your youth." (Eccl. 12:1). This is why, traditionally, so many young people were baptized while still in their teens and even younger.

tradition, the modern church has made the verification of salvation far too simple.

Before looking in greater detail at the conversion process as understood by African Baptists, it is necessary to say something about the language that describes that process. It will be seen throughout this chapter that the church's orally transmitted tradition has a theology and language that is unique to that religious heritage. It will be shown that the word "seek"—which is found more than eighty-five times in both the Old and New Testaments—takes on a whole new meaning; one that is radically different than what it is generally thought to mean.

Moreover, when doing word studies of the Hebrew and Greek languages, a word can have multiple meanings in English. For example, the word "seek" can mean *to search out, to strive after, to ask, to beg, to enquire, to desire, to discover that which is hidden.* The words of the prophets often warn Israel to "seek the Lord" in order to avert God's judgment. . "Seek the Lord while He may be found,...." says the Prophet Isaiah.[242] "Seek the Lord and live...." declares the Prophet Amos.[243]

It is necessary to seek after God not only that we may live, but also because He is *hidden.* The prophet Isaiah says of God: "Truly you are God, who hides

---

242 Is. 55:6.

243 Amos 5:6.

Yourself...."[244] Because God represents a hidden reality, it is necessary to seek after Him in the hope of finding Him. We find Jesus emphasizing similar words, "...seek, and you shall find;...."[245] Like the word "seek" the word "find" can have several meanings in English: *to perceive, to obtain, to discover, to gain awareness.* We will soon look at what transpires when one finds the Lord.

The Prophet Jeremiah declared, "Let not the wise man glory in his wisdom, let not the mighty man glory in his might, nor let the rich man glory in his riches; but let him who glories glory in this, that he understands and knows Me...."[246] It is this kind of *knowing* that is deeply personal, experiential, and intimate. The spiritual emptiness and lack of vision that characterize much of our worship can be attributed to our not *knowing* God. There would be less personality clashes and strained relationships if all members shared a common religious experience. As one elder recently stated, "When one has not prayed, it shows." It shows in our demeanour, in our walk and talk. Not knowing God personally (i.e.,

---

244 Is. 45:15. The Greek philosopher Plato wrote that "the god and maker of this world is

hard to find, but once you have found him to declare him unto all is impossible." (Timaeus, VII).

245 Matt. 7:7. I have read this verse of scripture several times but it was only after having a dream that it began to make sense. (As will be shown, dreams, visions, and voices are an integral part of the church's oral tradition.)

246 Jer. 9: 23--24.

experientially) helps to explain why our prayers often go unanswered. God does not hear our prayers if we do not know Him.

Knowing God results in a mutual relationship. Not only does the seeker know God, but God knows the seeker. It is to be "in Christ" and Christ "in me". And even after one has found God, you continue seeking. St. Paul expresses this reciprocal knowing and being known, when he writes: "Now I know in part, but then I shall know just as I also am known."[247] One not only knows God, but equally "known by God...."[248] The implications of not knowing God are expressed in the words of Jesus when, on the *Day of Judgment*, He will declare, "I never knew you...."[249] Even if one is able to quote chapter and verse from Genesis to Revelation, it is knowing Christ through the "indwelling" of His Spirit that one is saved— not how much Scriptural knowledge one may have acquired. Because God represents a hidden reality we cannot *know* Him objectively. This thought may have been expressed by a former southern slave in the nineteenth-century, but is still relevant today: "Nobody," he stated, "can talk about the religion of God unless you've had a conversion experience."[250]

In setting out to seek and to find God, the right mental attitude is necessary and requires a certain

---

247 1 Cor. 13:12.

248 Gal. 4:9.

249 Matt. 7:23.

250 Albert J. Raboteau, op. cit., 268.

mindset. Such an approach begins with a spirit of remorse, and the humble, contrite recognition of one's lost and sinful state—that one is a "hell-deserving sinner" in need of a Saviour, rather than one being a gift to the church. It is to recognize the need for forgiveness. Nothing offends the modern mind more than having to acknowledge "I am a sinner." A generation ago, there was greater respect and reverence for the spiritual wisdom of the elders. Such wisdom has since been lost in the present generation. Elders are certainly reverenced and respected, but not for their spiritual wisdom.

The stubborn and persistent nature of human pride does not easily yield to having to bow before a God who has claims upon us and demands accountability. All human effort and self-reliance must therefore be abandoned. One may be tempted to put forth rational arguments against such claims when what is required is self-surrender and total submission. For the gospel is not only one of proclamation, but one of *judgment!*

Several factors may contribute to one's decision to seek the Lord. There are the guilt feelings and subtle pressures to pray—to get your soul saved. It may be the result of the paralyzing fear of going to hell after hearing a powerful fire and brimstone message. It may result from someone else setting out to pray: a brother, sister, or friend or having had some near-death experience or the loss of a friend or loved one.

In the oral tradition, once a person has made the decision to pray, the next step is to tell someone of that decision, someone who has had a similar conversion experience. People who were interviewed for this project usually said it was their mother who guided them, who told them what to say. It could also be a relative, neighbour, or church member.

The second step calls for a certain discipline and a period of seclusion. It requires withdrawing from all worldly and familiar surroundings (i.e., family, friends, media, social gatherings, amusements, and secular allurements). In the words of that famous 1896 hymn "I Surrender All": "Worldly pleasures all forsaken." In some instances, it might even mean not attending school. Adults who set out to pray but who were employed and found themselves getting behind "they would have to catch-up", stated one elder.

Such detachment—not unlike the practice of the great Christian mystics—allows one to concentrate exclusively on God and one's lost state. It would often involve taking solitary walks and finding a sacred space sometimes in the woods, or church cemetery. It is here that one enters into a sustained period of prayer, lasting for several days or weeks; depending on the sincerity and seriousness of the seeker. One was encouraged to sleep as little as possible for fear of forgetting what one had seen or heard.[251] These nocturnal experiences are often expressed through dreams, visions, and voices.[252]

The individual setting out to find the Lord is instructed to repeat the following prayers:

- *Lord be merciful unto me a Sinner.*
- *Save my soul from hell, for Jesus' sake.*
- *Teach me how to pray.*
- *Wash me from my sin.*
- *Wash me in your blood...purge me, oh, Lord!*

---

251 There is great emphasis on feelings and how one is feeling when seeking the Lord. The nature of feelings in this context, however, are not mere fleeting, subjective emotions, as feelings are often described. Rather, the content of such feelings is understood as the moving and promptings of the Holy Spirit: feelings that are independent of the individual.

252 Given the limited scope of this project, it does not allow for a fuller discussion on dreams and visions. However, it should be said that the importance of dreams and visions is not unique to the African Baptist oral tradition. Since the dawn of human history, dreams, visions and voices have been seen as communicating with the Divine (with the gods). It has been said that dreams are the language of the soul (Jung). Not only are dreams and visions a great source of knowledge, wisdom, and inspiration, they are God's way of communicating with us mortals and making known His will. Nowhere is this more evident than in the Biblical narratives. The telling of Jesus' birth is communicated through dreams. Dreams are not only a source of information, but they tell us things we would not otherwise know. They warn us of certain dangers, what to avoid, and how we ought to live. But because of the often irrational and chaotic nature of dream images, interpretation is sometimes necessary to our understanding. It has been said that Albert Einstein discovered the *Law of Relativity* through a dream. (Jeremy Taylor, Dream Work (Paulist Press, New York 1983), 7.

- *Deliver my soul.*
- *Forgive my sins.*
- *In Jesus' name I pray.*

If this time of fervent and passionate seeking can be sustained, other prayers would then follow. William James perhaps describes accurately the experience and meaning of prayer, when he writes, "The act of prayer is no vain exercise of words, no mere repetition of sacred formulae, but the very movement itself of the soul, putting itself in a personal relation...with the mysterious power of which it feels the presence...."[253] Moreover, it is being in the presence of a mysterious power upon whom one's life depends. After entering into the presence of God through continued prayer and the confessing of one's sins, one begins to have experiences of seeing, hearing, and feeling. This will also be a time of great trial, temptation, and demonic distractions. In seeking the Lord, there is a heightened awareness and sensitivity to demonic spirits. Things that would not normally cross one's path will soon appear in various guises. This is an indication that one is on the

---

253 William James, op. cit., 352.

right track. If such intense, rigorous discipline cannot be maintained, many find themselves *turning back*.[254]

Depending on what one has *seen, heard,* or *felt,* the deacons were then summoned to question and examine the potential candidate.[255] Deacons were often skilled in dream interpretation and their meaning. And if the candidate is able to answer a series of questions based on their dreams and visions to the satisfaction of the deacons, the candidate was then ready to speak to the church membership. If, however, it is felt that the individual was not ready to speak to the congregation, they were encouraged to continue seeking. The decision that an individual is not ready is based on the fact that the seeker has not seen certain things when sharing their

---

254 Many who set out to pray soon discontinue when it is realized what is required. Had there been a greater understanding of what it means to "wait on God" as the scriptures show, many would have been less inclined to turn back. God always brings the seeker to the place where one is forced to wait. The author attempted to pray at the early age of sixteen, but quickly abandoned the effort. The attempt was made again at twenty-three and was successful.

255 Many people take issue today with someone deciding when they are ready to be baptized. No one they feel has that right. In the past it was the sole responsibility of the deacons who determined whether an individual was ready to be baptized.

experience—the most important being the blood of Christ—without which there was no salvation![256]

If one has not met with the deacon's approval, a second visit is necessary. Once it is agreed that the seeker is *out*—a term meaning one has found the Lord—the individual is then ready to tell his/her experience. Depending on the time of year a person prays, the seeker may speak to the church two or three times before his/her baptism. There was the expectation that each time a candidate spoke, they were to have something different to tell the church. If the seeker did not have something new to report, it was thought that the candidate was "playing not praying." The candidate would then be admonished to continue seeking and to "watch and pray!"

One of the questions asked to ascertain the authenticity of the candidate's conversion was "If the church did not accept or believe your experience, what would you say? The response usually was "I know what God has done for me even if you do not accept

---

256 The importance and role of the blood in the conversion experience bears repeating. The centrality and significance of the blood can be seen throughout both the Old and New Testaments (Gen. 4:10, 9:4, Ex. 12:13, 24:8, Lev. 17:11, 14, Num. 19:17, 35:33, Matt. 26:28, 27:24,25, Jn. 6:54, Acts17:26, Rom 3:25, 5:9, Col. 1:14, Heb. 9:22, 1 Jn. 5:8) Its redemptive power can be seen in many of the great hymns of the church. The blood of Christ is the foundation upon which the church's oral tradition rests. It represents new life and a new beginning. The blood connotes origins and the place from where one proceeds. It is through the blood that the spirit is *tested* to determine "whether it is of God" (1 Jn, 4:1).

it." Another question was whether the candidate was on speaking terms with everyone. If there was someone with whom the candidate was not speaking, he/she was required to go and be reconciled with that person before giving their experience.[257] Jesus pointed out this important principle of reconciliation when He stated, "Therefore if you bring your gift to the altar, and there remember that your brother has something against you, leave your gift there before the altar....First be reconciled to your brother, and then come and offer your gift."[258] What this passage suggests is that human relationships (how we treat one another) is as important as worshipping God.

After hearing the candidate's experience, the congregation is asked whether it has any questions for the candidate. A vote is then called for. Someone then stands-up and says, "We accept the testimony of the [candidate] and that they are taken under the watch care of the church, not only until baptism but until death."[259] All those in favour of the motion are

---

257 The African Baptist oral tradition was not merely about one's salvation, but one is expected to display a Christian character. Whatever differences or disagreements that may have existed, once one is saved all differences are resolved.
258 Matt. 5:23, 24.

259 Once the individual has officially become a candidate for baptism, they are taken under the protective and watchful eye of the church. The new member's life is no longer one's own; one now belongs to the church and the family of God. The candidate must continue to seek the Lord and walk circumspect not just until baptism, but throughout the rest of life.

asked to stand. The motion is carried by a unanimous vote. Often with tears flowing and rapturous joy, the candidate is accompanied by someone to shake hands with all of the members. As this happens, the congregation strikes up an uplifting spiritual that "a sinner has come home!" This is then followed by a circle around the church to form what is called the "ring shout." With spontaneous jubilation, the members join hands with arms swinging in a back-and-forth motion to the spiritual "*I'm Gonna Shout, Shout, Shout...I'm Gonna Shout God's Harvest Over!...*"

What transpires when God finally reveals Himself, when one encounters and is touched by the power and holiness of God? According to the tradition, several things may occur, and no two experiences are ever the same.

First, there is an overwhelming sense of ineffable joy, which is one of the "fruits of the Spirit." It is what St. Paul calls the "newness of life."[260] However, St. Paul qualifies this statement by saying, *should* walk in newness of life. One is given a new lease on life, an opportunity to begin anew. When one has truly repented, it means making a 180-degree turn and going in the other direction; this is what repentance literally means. The burden of sin and guilt of one's former life is remembered no more. The bondage in which one was held is broken in principle if not in fact. For at every new level of moral achievement

---

260 Rom. 6:4.

sin will inevitably manifest itself. Christ represents the *new* (qualitatively new) creation.[261] It is the radical regeneration of the self and the shattering of the human ego, resulting in a new perspective and a new set of values. In short, it is to encounter the Risen Christ!

Secondly, one experiences the saving power of the blood, forgiveness of sin, and the infusion of God's grace—which are all synonymous with receiving the Holy Spirit. Put another way, to receive the Holy Spirit is to receive the gift of grace. Traditionally, grace has been defined as "God's unmerited favour." However, this definition (according to the oral tradition) does not go far enough, falling far short of the Biblical understanding of grace and its role in the life of the believer. According to the American pastor and theologian, Reinhold Niebuhr, "grace is the power of God over man." He continues: "...grace represents an accession of resources, which man does not have of himself, enabling him to become what he truly ought to be."[262] Grace as a spiritual power and resource (which Christ offers) runs throughout St. Paul's theology.[263] It is *grace* that saves us! All that St. Paul was able to accomplish, endured, and suffered, he attributed to God's grace: "...but I laboured more

---

261 2 Cor. 5:17.

262 Reinhold Niebuhr, *The Nature and Destiny of Man*, (Vol. 2, Charles Scribner's Son, New York, 1963), 99.

263 Rom. 1:5, 3:25, 1 Cor. 1:14, 15:10, Gal. 1:6, 2:9, Eph. 2:5, 8, 3:7.

abundantly than they all," he writes, "yet not I, but the grace of God which was with me."[264]

It is therefore through grace alone that one is saved, and not through good works or human effort. The failure to receive God's grace explains why many Christians bear little or no spiritual fruit in their lives and instead become detached spectators rather than active participants. It is preferable not to be baptized if an individual has not received the gift of *grace*, which was practised in the Preston churches. Far too many "graceless" Christians have come into the church.

One of the questions put to the candidate when sharing his/her experience with the church is, "Can any other blood save you?" This question shows the centrality and importance of the blood of Christ in the conversion process. The central role of the blood can also be seen in various New Testament passages.[265] Having been washed from our sin, one is now forgiven and justified. To experience the *blood*,

---

264 1 Cor. 15:10.

265 Lk. 22:20, Rom. 3:25, 5:9, Eph. 1:7, Col: 14, Heb. 13:12, 1Jn. 1:7, Rev. 7:14. Despite the many sermons preached on the role and importance of Christ's shed blood, there is still some confusion regarding this important church doctrine. Experiencing the power and blood of Christ, in fact, as over against recognizing and acknowledging it in principle, are radically different. One may accept the fact that Christ's shed blood washes away my sin, but yet never *experience* the washing away of one's sin. An analogous example is to say I believe in God, and yet not *know* God; the two are not synonymous.

therefore, is to receive grace, forgiveness, and the Holy Spirit.

In all three of the synoptic Gospels (Matthew 3:11, Mark 1:8, Luke 3:16), John the Baptist speaks of two baptisms: water baptism and the baptism of the Holy Ghost. We do not always make the distinction between water baptism and Holy Ghost baptism, (Holy Ghost and Holy Spirit is often used interchangeably). We all experience the symbolism of water baptism (i.e., the baptism of repentance for the remission of sins) when we first make a public confession of accepting Christ into our lives. Water baptism alone, however, does not produce the "newness of life." This can be seen in the lives of so many that have been baptized. St. Paul describes in Romans, chapter 7, in great detail the inner struggle that continues even after baptism.[266]

The baptism of the Holy Ghost (Holy Spirit), however, is a totally different matter. Understood as the Third Person of the Trinity, Jesus describes the Holy Ghost as the *Comforter* that He will send after his death and resurrection.[267] Translated as the "Paraclete" from the Greek word *Parakletos*, this word has several meanings. It literally means to come along side as a helper, intercessor, advocate, or counsel for the defence. The Holy Ghost acts as Christ's substitute in the world and intercedes on our behalf.

---

266 Rom. 7.

267 Jn. 16:7.

In receiving the Holy Ghost, one receives a certain *power*[268] which enables one to experience "newness of life." Experiencing the power of the Holy Ghost is experienced before water baptism. Moreover, it is an *experience* that cannot be self-produced but can only come as a result of *seeking*.

---

268 Acts 1:8.

Epilogue

Personal Reflections

I grew-up in the historic Black community of Cherry Brook, five miles east of the city of Dartmouth. My parents (who are both now deceased) were Ernest and Olive Mae (nee Thomas) Sparks. I had six siblings: five brothers and one sister. Both of my parents were Christians, but it was Mother who attended church regularly. She was a member of the choir and *Women's Missionary Society* (WMS). My father had become an usher six months before he passed in May 1982. We attended church along with our parents, and went to Sunday school until we were old enough to decide we no longer wanted to go.

Like most homes in the community, we had a family Bible, but it was seldom read. It was just there as a kind of fixture. There were no family devotions or religious discussions. We never said grace before meals. After I joined the church in 1975, we began holding cottage prayer meetings at our house. These were weekly house-to-house prayer/praise sessions led by the deacons and organized by Deaconess Kathleen Riley.

The thing that always caught my attention was the framed Bible verses on the walls. These scripture verses were there from the time I could remember. One verse in particular, which I recall memorizing, was Rom. 6:23: "For the wages of sin is death; but the gift of God is eternal life through Jesus Christ our Lord." Though I had memorized this verse, I had no idea what it meant nor had I ever bothered to enquire.

What I vividly remember about my mother was her different religious expressions, which I heard on an almost daily basis. For example, if she was planning to do something, she would always say, "If God spares life," she would do such and such. Another expression was: "God works in mysterious ways." Or if the name of a deceased person was mentioned, mom would say, "God bless." As I reflect now, I realize that mother was deeply pious. She had a certain moral character--a natural grace and goodness about her.

Despite this early Christian exposure and upbringing, I was never told about salvation or the need for baptism. Those types of conversations just did not come up. This was not unique to our family. None of my friends were getting baptized, and we never ever talked about God at home.

Yet without talking or discussing my decision with anyone, at the age of sixteen, I decided it was time to seek the Lord. I thought it was universal: that it was what everyone did and not unique to the Cherry Brook. I had only been praying for about three days when I decided I was not ready. I had decided to *turned back.*

Seven years later (1975), I would set out again to pray, only this time with greater success. On July 28, 1975, I entered the waters of baptism but not before becoming an atheist in those intervening years and trying to convince other Christians there was no God! I'm not sure what my parents would have thought of me had they known I thought this way.

By the time I turned 20, I had become a dyed-in-the-wool atheist. My faith was in "reason" and my ability to logically think things through for myself. I had become the *great rationalist!* I believed that man was indeed "the measure of all things." Nothing existed which could not be rationally understood or explained. Given that God's existence could not be rationally proven, He must, therefore, not exist. Nothing existed beyond the five senses. The idea of hell was inconceivable. In my naiveté I believed Earth was hell. Reason would not permit me to think of a place more evil than planet Earth.

Armed with prideful reason, I was on a mission to destroy the belief in God's existence. I debated with such passion and persuasiveness that I convinced my Christian friends that there was no God. No one was able to convince me otherwise or even bothered to do so. I continued with my atheistic mission for about three years.

Then in January 1975, I began to have a change of mind—and heart. While living in one room at 57 Prince Albert Road and unemployed, I started reading the Bible, beginning with Genesis. Why this change came about at this particular time I am at a loss to explain. There was no sudden revelation or flash of insight. As I now reflect on that period of my life, it was not that I suddenly started believing. Merely believing that God existed was not enough. Rather, I wanted to challenge my unbelief. If there was a God, I wanted to *know* with absolute certainty. I wanted to know Him personally! Simply believing would not give me this certainty. Hence, I continued reading the Bible, more out of curiosity than conviction.

In the spring of 1975, I felt myself being miraculously changed. My conversations with Christians took on a different tone. I was no longer the rationalist that I had been. Instead, I was now seriously considering getting baptized, even though I was not yet a candidate. My friends did not know what to think. But here I was telling people I was going to be baptized that summer. I was determined to pray and be ready for baptism by July of that year.

I went to visit my parents to ask if I could move back home, that "I wanted to try and pray." I did not share with them my atheistic unbelief. They willingly agreed. There is nothing that brings greater joy to parents than seeing their children set out to pray. This is particularly the case if one is the first to do so. In the first week of July 1975, I began seeking the Lord at the age of twenty-three. I would marry the former Sylvia Crawley three weeks before my baptism.

Mother was very helpful in telling me what to say and how I ought to pray. She advised me to "go to God in earnest." Seeing myself as a hell-deserving sinner in need of a Saviour, I prayed more earnestly to God. As I continued praying and asking God for forgiveness and to have mercy upon me, other prayers began flowing from my lips.

I had been praying for about a week before I started seeing certain dreams and visions. I had not experienced dreams up until this time. In those dreams, I saw myself in different situations and places and saw certain people. I was told there were certain things I had to *see* before the deacons would come to examine me—one of those things was the blood of Christ.

Now into my second week, the deacons were called to hear what I had seen and experienced. I was told I was not ready, but was "on the right track" and that I should "continue to pray". With guilt feelings, remorseful, and many tears, I continued seeking. I spent many hours in solitude and taking long walks.

Finally, my breakthrough came in the third week as I was sitting in my father's car. It was around midnight. Suddenly, I felt light-hearted and filled with ineffable joy. Not being able to contain myself, I quickly got out of the car and began running around the yard, jumping about a foot off the ground. Not fully understanding just what was transpiring, I made a sudden dash for the house to tell mother how I was feeling. Both mom and dad by this time were in bed. I ran up stairs and knocked on the door. Coming to the door, I threw my arms around Mother and cried out, "I found the Lord!!!"

The God whom I had denied existed and blasphemed had revealed Himself to me. I had received His Spirit! I thought of the Apostle Paul, who had been a blasphemer but obtained mercy because he did it through ignorance and unbelief; I too had obtained God's mercy despite my ignorance and unbelief. I had come to see that there were no rational arguments for God's existence, but only having "a humble and contrite heart." The memory of my experience continues to be an ongoing blessing.

My conversion experience created within me an unquenchable thirst for spiritual wisdom and knowledge. I preached my first sermon on September 15 of that year at Cherry Brook. I would go on to preach a total of thirteen times in the first year following my conversion. I was now proclaiming that which I had vigorously denied. My mind and intellect were now in the service of the Master who died in my place! In the fall of 1981—six years after my conversion—I enrolled in the *Bachelor of Theology* program at Acadia Divinity College.

Going to college not having finished high school, but as a mature student at the age of twenty-eight, would prove a daunting task. Throughout my first year I was constantly gripped by the fear of failure. But through God's grace I was able to complete five courses in my freshman year. In the years that followed, my workload would become less burdensome. University life opened up for me a whole new world, but it was not without what Luther called the "dark night of the soul." These were moments of intense spiritual agony when I did not think I could continue. I recall going to my New Testament professor and sharing with him my spiritual battles and that I was "considering dropping out". He encouraged me to continue.

Refreshed and revived by the words of my professor, I pressed forward. Yet I soon found myself drifting back into my former state and eventually dropped out of college in my second year only to return again for the next fall semester. In 1985 I would drop out again. I would not return to Acadia until 1992 when I would finally complete my degree. "To God be the glory great things He has done!"

Conclusion

This book traces the development and evolution of the African Baptist Church from its humble beginnings in the slave cabins of the American South to its establishment in Nova Scotia by Loyalist preacher, the Reverend David George. This study attempts to show how what was first transmitted orally became organized and institutionalized. One of the great short comings in researching and documenting an oral tradition is that it fails to fully capture and express the true nature and character of that tradition. Moreover, because such a tradition is of a sacred origin, existing since time immemorial, such research must in some ways remain incomplete.

The ABC as an organized religion (and like organized religion generally) results in the stultifying and suppression of the Holy Spirit. Believing itself to be worshipping God, the church has become "self-worship." Coupled with self-worship is the false notion that God is always blessing us. Church members are expected to conform and to follow the same script. Loyalty is to the pastor or the church, rather than to

Jesus the Christ. This is the nature and character of organized religion.

This study has attempted to show the Christian and Biblical roots of the church's dynamic oral tradition. Moreover, this work has sought to challenge and clarify many misconceptions and distortions of the church's oral history. It endeavours to challenge the conventional and contemporary approach to salvation now so prevalent within African Baptist circles. Further, it seeks to challenge the church's out-dated theology.

It is hoped that this work will begin a conversation and theological dialogue among the faithful. At a time when the influence of organized religion is waning in Canada (according to the latest Reid Poll, April '22), and may in fact be "doing more harm than good." The church universal is facing a host of challenges—not the less of which is a credibility crisis.

Finally, the Church must guard itself against secular influences that are entering the Church (e.g., Africentricity): a world-view that runs counter to the Christian world-view. We cannot have it both ways. It is either/or not both/and.

It is against this backdrop that we must revisit, rediscover, and reclaim the African Baptist oral tradition.

Bibliography

Armstrong, Maurice. *The Great Awakening in Nova Scotia*. Connecticut: The American Society of Church History, 1948.

Bill, I.E. *Fifty Years With the Baptist Ministers and Churches of the Maritime Provinces of Canada*. New Brunswick: Barnes and Company, 1880.

Boles, John B. *Masters & Slaves in the House of the Lord*. Kentucky: University Press of Kentucky, 1988.

Clark, Erskine *Westlin' Jacob: A Portrait of Religion in the Old South*. Kentucky: John Knox Press, 1941.

Cramp, J.M. *The Baptist of Nova Scotia, 1760–1860*. Nova Scotia: Acadia University, Special Collections.

Davidson, Stephen Eric. *Black Loyalists in New Brunswick: The Lives of Eight African Americans in Colonial New Brunswick 1783-1834*. Nova Scotia: Formac Publishing Co., Ltd., 2020.

Frazier, Franklin. *The Negro Church in America*. New York: Schocken Books, 1963.

Gallay, Alan. *Planters and Slaves in the Great Awakening*. Mississippi: Journal of Southern History, 1978.

Genovese, Eugene. *Roll, Jordon, Roll: The World The Slave Made*. New York: Pantheon, 1974.

Gordon, Grant. *From Slavery to Freedom: The Life of David George, Pioneer Black Baptist Minister*. Nova Scotia: Lancelot Press Ltd., 1992.

Hopkins, Dwight H. *Down Up and Over: Slave Religion and Black Theology*. Minnesota: Fortress Press, 2000.

James, William. *The Varieties of Religious Experience*. New York: The New American Library, Inc., 1958.

Kierkegaard, Soren. *Concluding Unscientific Postscript*. New Jersey: Princeton University Press, 1941.

Levine, Lawrence W. *Black Culture and Black Consciousness: Afro-American Folk Thought from Slavery to Freedom*. New York: Oxford University Press, 1977.

Levy, George Edward. *The Baptists of the Maritime Provinces*. New Brunswick: Barnes-Hopkins Ltd., 1947

Lincoln C. Eric and Mamiya Lawrence H. *The Black Church in the African American Experience*. Durham and London: Duke University Press, 1990.

Matthews, Donald G. *Religion in the Old South*. Illinois: University of Chicago Press, 1979.

Mays, Benjamin Elijah, Nicholson and Joseph William *The Negro's Church*.

New York: Russell & Russell, 1933.

McKerrow, Peter E. *A Brief History of Blacks in Nova Scotia* (Ed. By Frank S. Boyd). Nova Scotia: Nova Scotia Printing Co., 1895.

Niebuhr, Reinhold. *The Nature and Destiny of Man*. New York: Charles Scribner's Son, 1963.

Oliver, Pearleen. *A Brief History of the Colored Baptists of Nova Scotia 1783-1953*.

Booklet Published In Commemoration of the Centenary of the African United Baptist Association of Nova Scotia. Nova Scotia: AUBA, 1953.

Pachai, Bridglal. *Beneath the Clouds of the Promise Land*: The *Survival of Nova Scotia's Blacks, Vol 1 & 2*. Nova Scotia: Lancelot Press Ltd., 1990.

Paris, Peter J. *The Social Teachings of the Black Churches*. Pennsylvania: Fortress Press, 1985.

The Spirituality of African People: The Search for a Moral Discourse. Minnesota: Fortress Press, 1995.

Raboteau, Albert J. *Slave Religion: The Invisible Institution in the Antebellum South*. New York: Oxford University Press, 1978.

Richey, Matthew. *Memoir of Reverend William Black*. Nova Scotia: Baldwin Collection of Canadiana, 1839.

Rippon, John. *The Baptist Annual Register 1790-1793*. Kentucky: Southern Baptist Theological Seminary Library, 2019.

Sernett, Milton C.. *Black Religion and American Evangelicalism*. New Jersey:

The Scarecrow Press, Inc., 1975.

Sobel, Mechal. *Trabelin' On: The Slave Journey To An Afro-Baptist Faith*. Connecticut: Greenwood Press, 1979.

Taylor, Jeremy. *Dream Work*. New York: Paulist Press, 1983.

Thomas, Thomas, Duncan, Ray, Jr., and Westfield. *Black Church Studies*. Tennessee: Abingdon Press, 200.7

Toynbee, Arnold J. *A Study of History*. New York: Oxford University Press, 1947.

Walker, James W. St. G. *The Black Loyalists: The Search for a Promise Land in Nova Scotia and*

Sierra Leone 1783-1870. Nova Scotia: Dalhousie University Press, 1975.

Wilmore, Guyraud S. *Black Religion and Black Radicalism.* New York: Double Day & Co., 1972.

Winks, Robin W. *The Blacks in Canada: A History.* Quebec: McGill-Queens's University Press, 1971.

Young, Henry J. *Major Black Religious Leaders 1755-1940.* Tennessee: Abingdon Press, 1983.

Additional Sources

Allwood, Philip G.A.. *First Baptist Church. Its Origins and Early Years*.Master of Divinity Thesis, Acadia University, Wolfville, NS, 1978.

Annual Minutes of the *African Baptist Association*, 1869, 1903, 1917.

Bailey, Constance. *Give Me That Old-Time Religion: Reclaiming Slave Religion in the future*. Maters Thesis, University of Missouri-Columbia, 2007.

Black Loyalist.com.

Cook, Matthew W. *The Impact of Revivalism on Baptist Faith and Practise in the American South Prior to the Civil War*. Ph. D. Dissertation, Baylor University, Waco, Tx, 2009.

Cherry Brook United Baptist Church 90th Anniversary Booklet 1902-1992. Cherry Brook, Nova Scotia, 1992.

Davidson, Stephen Eric. *Leaders of the Black Baptists of Nova Scotia 1782-1832*. Thesis for Bachelor of Arts Degree, Honours, Acadia University, Wolfville, NS, 1975.

Memoir of Boston King, Methodist Magazine. 1798.

PBS.org/*This Far by Faith*.

Peter Randolph's *Autobiography*. 1893.

Perez, Susel's essay on *Slavery in the Western Hemisphere*, 2010.